TALES
from the
DUAL MONARCHY

*Twenty short stories
from Austria-Hungary*

BLUE DANUBE

BLUE
DANUBE

An imprint of Somerset Books, Budapest
Distributed by Blue Guides Limited of London
Distributed in the USA by WW Norton & Company, Inc.
500 Fifth Avenue, New York, NY 10110

Tales from the Dual Monarchy
Twenty short stories from Austria-Hungary
Translated by Annabel Barber
Somerset Books 2025

Translation © Annabel Barber 2025
All rights reserved. No part of these translations
may be reproduced, stored in a retrieval system or transmitted in
any form or by any means without permission of the publishers.

ISBN 978-1-916568-07-5

Front cover: *Falling Leaves* by Philip de Laszlo (1895),
photo Tibor Mester © de Laszlo Foundation / Hungarian National Gallery.

Every effort has been made to contact the copyright owners
of material reproduced in this book. We would be pleased to hear
from any copyright owners we have been unable to reach.

Printed and bound in Hungary by Dürer Nyomda Kft., Gyula.
somersetbooks.com/bluedanube

Author images (Unless otherwise stated, images are from Wikimedia Commons): Endre Ady: 1908 photo by Aladár Székely; Géza Csáth: photo c. 1915; Marie von Ebner-Eschenbach: 1873 portrait by Karl von Blaas; Egid Filek von Wittinghausen: from *Deutsch-Österreichische Literaturgeschichte*, 1937; Elek Gozsdu: 1905 portrait by Károly Kernstok; Hugo von Hofmannsthal: 1910 photo by Nicola Perscheid; Margit Kaffka: 1912 photo by Aladár Székely; Dezső Kosztolányi: 1935 photo by Aladár Székely; Károly Lovik: photo from 1915; Kálmán Mikszáth: 1910 portrait by Gyula Benczúr; Zsigmond Móricz: Fortepan, photo from 1940; Rainer Marie Rilke: photo from 1900; Alexander Roda Roda: 1910 photo by Hugo Erfurth; Joseph Roth: photo from 1926; Richard Schaukal: 1924 photo by Hermann Kosel; Arthur Schnitzler: 1912 photo by Ferdinand Schmutzer; Cécile Tormay: unknown date; László Tóth: photo from 1929; Stefan Zweig: photo from 1900.

Inside front cover image: Fortepan /Róbert Keresztesy
Inside back cover image: Fortepan / Budapest Főváros Levéltára / Klösz György fényképei.

Contents

Introduction   9

The Austrians

Hugo von Hofmannsthal: Justice   13

Rainer Maria Rilke: The Runaway   17

Arthur Schnitzler: The Greek Dancer   24

Egid Filek von Wittinghausen: The Glass Door   39

Stefan Zweig: The Star Above the Trees   47

Richard Schaukal: Andreas von Balthesser to Countess F—   59

Alexander Roda Roda: The Consequences of a Non-Regulation Collar   66

Marie von Ebner-Eschenbach: The Poetry of the Unwitting   75

Therese Rie: A Petty Bourgeoise   92

Joseph Roth: Something Ever Rarer   120

The Hungarians

Kálmán Mikszáth: Lőrinc's Hats	127
Elek Gozsdu: Autumn Rain	134
Margit Kaffka: Madam and Miss	143
Endre Ady: Juliette Goes to Florence	156
Zsigmond Móricz: Seven Farthings	162
Károly Lovik: The Silent Crime	170
Dezső Kosztolányi: The Cabaret Singer's Miraculous Comeback	183
Géza Csáth: Little Emma	193
Cécile Tormay: The Golden Snake	205
László Tóth: Ministry of Justice	214
The authors	226
Notes	237

Translator's note

This collection comprises twenty short stories, either set or written during the Austro-Hungarian Empire's period of greatest splendour and prosperity, from c. 1885 to its collapse after the First World War. The final story in each section is the exception, being written after the Empire had disintegrated, and harking back to it with a measure of irony and nostalgia. There has been no criterion for selection beyond that of each story being one I have enjoyed reading. Some of the authors are well known; others, as far as I know, have not been translated into English before.

AB

Acknowledgements

With grateful thanks to László Czirják, György Spiró, Sandra de Laszlo, Christopher Wentworth Stanley.

Introduction

It wasn't a bad deal, all in all, while it lasted. Inevitably, better for some than for others, but with more than a dozen languages, it's difficult to keep everyone happy. For instance, you might end up dangerously obsessed with a Polish Countess, as in Stefan Zweig's story 'The Star Above the Trees'.

The Dual Monarchy of Austria-Hungary was formed in 1867, on the basis of a 'compromise'. The Hungarian revolution of 1848–9 against the Habsburg monarchy had been crushed, brutally, not by the Austrians, but by Russian troops summoned in. The Austrians were thrashed by the Prussians in 1866. The idea of just getting along with each other suddenly became very enticing.

The Austrians bought off the Hungarians, the dominant ethnic group in their empire, hoping to keep the Czechs, Croats, Serbs and others in line. It worked for half a century, until a Bosnian Serb assassin gunned down the heir to the throne in Sarajevo.

With hindsight, the Dual Monarchy was an era of emboldened culture, and of ruthless education. It coincided with the *belle époque* in France (after the Prussians defeated the French in 1871). Europe was awash with new ideas, many of them Paris-based. Rainer Maria Rilke, Endre Ady and almost every Central European creator was obliged to hang out on the Left Bank. Paris had the painters—Paris did the decorating for the twentieth century—but the Danube Boys (and a handful of girls), from Vienna and Budapest, often Jewish, often emigrated, were ultimately to have a more profound influence in matters of science, technology and economics. Check the Nobel Laureates list.

In this collection, ten stories by Austrian writers are presented side by side with ten stories by Hungarians. There is irony, world-weariness, cynicism, complacency, and a lack of awareness of how close to the brink of collapse their world was. Nevertheless, most of the stories here reflect that sense of Habsburg stability and order, maybe too much order (as in Alexander Roda Roda's story). It is also interesting to compare the styles of the two groups. The Hungarian stories (and others of that period) often have a playful quality. Kálmán Mikszáth's story about hats fits into a huge genre of antics in cafés. Károly Lovik's contribution is, of course, a grimmer twist on pranking.

Endre Ady is best known as a poet, not a prose writer, but he is almost a comedian compared to his poetic successors, who wrote some of the bleakest poetry of the twentieth century as Hungary suffered misfortune after misfortune. The Austrians were very keen on starting the First World War. The Hungarians were not, but they were to suffer the penalties for being on the losing side.

This collection offers a judicious mix of the celebrated and the insufficiently celebrated. Readers are quite likely to think of Arthur Schnitzler when they think of Vienna; but when they turn to Hungary, they're less likely to think of

Margit Kaffka, who lived much of her life in the provinces and who died young in the Influenza outbreak of 1918. Both Schnitzler and Kaffka offer a dissection of marriage that will ring true to contemporary readers and agony aunts (and Schnitzler—almost as you would expect from the boss of Viennese decadence—also throws in some cross-dressing).

Tibor Fischer
Budapest, 2025

Hugo von Hofmannsthal
JUSTICE

I was sitting in the middle of the garden. In front of me, the gravel path led up between two pale green patches of grass to a point where the hill erupted skywards and the palings of the dark green picket fence were sharply silhouetted against the blue. It was springtime. The path ended at a little gate. Bees hovered in the soft, transparent air, flitting here and there among the pale pink peach blossom.

Suddenly, a rattling was heard from the little gate and a dog came bounding into the garden: a tall, fragile, long-legged greyhound. Behind the dog came an angel: a young, slim, blonde angel, one of God's slender heralds. He wore pointy-toed shoes; a long sword hung by his side and he carried a dagger in his belt. His chest and shoulders were clad in finely wrought, steel-grey armour on which the sunlight danced, and petals from the peach trees were falling into his long, thick, golden hair. Closing the gate behind him, he started up the gravel path towards me, a supple figure in an emerald green doublet. The sleeves were puffed from shoulder to elbow, while from elbow to wrist they were close-fitting, revealing delicate, well-formed hands. Slowly, gracefully, he approached, his left hand playing with the hilt of his dagger. The dog trotted alongside its master, every now and again looking up at him lovingly.

The angel was very close by now, about the same distance as a five-year-old child can throw a ball. Will he speak to me? I wondered.

On the lawn, the gardener's boy was playing with the fallen petals. He toddled across to the angel and stood staring at his feet.

'What lovely shoes you have!' he said.

'Yes,' said the angel, 'I have. They are cut from the mantle of the Mother of God.'

I noticed then that they were made of cloth of gold, with red flowers or possibly fruits picked out amongst the weave.

'The holy Apostle Peter once ran after the Mother of God,' said the angel to the child, 'because he wanted to tell her something. But she didn't stop when he called because she hadn't heard him. So he ran after her, and in his haste, he trod on her train and a piece of it came away. And so she stopped wearing that mantle and it was used instead to make shoes for us all.'

'The shoes are very beautiful,' said the child again.

The angel continued on his way down the gravel path. This meant that inevitably he must pass my bench. An inexpressible joy came over me at the idea that he might speak to me, too. Because the words that he uttered seemed to be clothed in a kind of radiance. It was as if, as he uttered them, he was thinking of something else entirely; as if he were dreaming of heavenly bliss, with a private, covert rejoicing.

By now, the angel was standing right in front of me. I doffed my hat in greeting and stood to my feet. But when I looked up, I shrank back in fear at the expression on his face.

His features were sublimely beautiful but the blue eyes held a dark, almost threatening fire, and there was nothing mortal about that golden hair, which had a faintly sinister, metallic sheen. Beside him stood the dog, one forepaw delicately raised, looking at me with its keen eyes.

'Are you a just man?' asked the angel sternly.

His tone was haughty, almost disdainful.

I attempted a smile. 'I'm not a bad man. I'm fond of a good many people. The world is full of beautiful things.'

'Are you *just*?' asked the angel again. It was as if he had not heard what I said. There was a hint of lordly impatience in his tone; he sounded like a master repeating an order to a servant who has not fully understood what is required of him. He grasped the dagger in his right hand and drew it a little way out of its sheath. I began to feel afraid. I tried to work out the purport of his question, but I couldn't; my head was in a whirl, incapable of fathoming the meaning of his words. My mind came up against a blank wall. Frantically, I tried to force myself to think.

'I have seen so little of life,' I said at last. 'But sometimes a powerful feeling of love gusts through me, and nothing seems strange or inexplicable when that happens. At times like that, I am sure that I am just, because I feel as if I can comprehend everything: how the earth throws up the whispering trees and how the stars hang and spin in space; the deepest essence of everything, down to all the doings of little men...'

I felt myself quail before the scorn in the angel's eyes. A horrible awareness of my inadequacy came over me and I knew that I was blushing for shame. The expression in those eyes clearly said: 'What a contemptible, vacuous babbler!' There was not a trace of mercy or pity in his tone. A haughty smile played about his narrow lips. He turned to go.

'Justice is everything,' he said. 'Justice is first, justice is last. He who does not understand this will perish.'

So saying, he turned and walked away, going back down the path with elastic tread, vanishing briefly behind the honeysuckle bower, then emerging again, and finally descending the stone steps, disappearing in stages, first the slender legs from ankle to knee, then the hips, then the armour-plated shoulders, and finally the golden hair and the emerald green cap. Behind him ran the dog. It hovered for a while on the top step, in graceful, sharp outline, before leaping, in a single bound, into the void, into invisibility.

Geregtichkeit. 1893

Rainer Maria Rilke
THE RUNAWAY

The church was completely empty. Through the brightly coloured stained-glass window above the high altar came a shaft of evening light, bold and direct, the way such shafts of light are always depicted by Old Masters in images of the Annunciation. It shone into the nave and kindled new colour in the faded carpet that covered the chancel steps. The Baroque wooden uprights of the rood screen divided the space in two; beyond them, everything seemed sunk in gathering gloom and the small oil lamps flickered ever more indulgently in front of the sombre saints.

Behind the last crude sandstone column at the very back of the church sat a boy and a girl, with one of the carved panels of the Stations of the Cross suspended directly above them. The pale-faced girl seemed to be squeezing her light brown jacket into the furthest corner of the heavy, black oak pew. The rose in her hat tickled the chin of the wooden angel on the carved backrest, making him smile. The boy, Fritz, a grammar school student, held the girl's hands in both his own; two tiny hands in threadbare gloves. He held them just as one might hold a nestling bird, gently and yet secure. He was happy.

They will lock the church, he thought. They'll lock it without noticing us, and then we'll be all alone. I'm sure the church is haunted at night.

They huddled closer together and Anna whispered anxiously, 'It's getting quite late, isn't it?'

A gloomy vision immediately rose in both their minds. In hers, it was an image of the place where she sat sewing, day in-day out. All she could see was a blank, ugly fire wall; never a glimpse of sunlight. In Fritz's mind rose a vision of his desk, strewn with Latin textbooks and an open copy of Plato's *Symposium*. They both stared straight ahead and their gazes came to rest at the same point, tracing the grooves and runnels of the altar rail.

They looked into each other's eyes and Anna sighed.

Quietly and protectively, Fritz put his arm around her and said, 'If only we could go away!'

Anna glanced at him and saw the desire that burned in his eyes. She lowered her lids and blushed.

Fritz went on, 'I loathe them all. I utterly loathe them! You should see how they look at me when they know I've been with you. They are nothing but a mass of suspicion and malice. But I'm not a child any more. As soon as I can earn some money, we'll go away together, far away. We'll defy them all.'

'Do you love me?' The pale girl waited for his answer.

'I can't begin to describe how much I love you.' And Fritz kissed the question from her lips.

'How soon will it be before you can take me away with you?' the girl asked tentatively.

Fritz said nothing. Involuntarily, he raised his eyes, followed the outline of the crude sandstone column and saw the inscription above the Station of the Cross where they were sitting: 'Father, forgive them…'

'Does your family suspect anything?' he asked, suddenly angry. 'Tell me,' he insisted.

Dumbly, Anna nodded.

'So they do!' he fumed. 'Oh—those gossips! If only I could…' He buried his head in his hands.

Anna leaned her head against his shoulder. 'Don't take on so,' she said softly.

They sat like that for some time. Then, suddenly, Fritz looked up and said, 'Come away with me!'

Anna forced a smile into her beautiful eyes, which by now were full of tears. Helplessly, she shook her head. And once again, Fritz clasped her hands, her tiny hands in their worn-out gloves. He looked up the long nave. The sun had faded now and the stained-glass windows were nothing more than dull, colourless patches. There was total silence.

Then, from somewhere far above their heads, came a high-pitched sound. They both looked up and saw a lost little swallow, frantically seeking the open air with tired, bewildered wings.

On his way home, Fritz remembered a piece of Latin homework he had failed to hand in. He decided to apply himself to his books, despite his lack of interest and his fatigue. But somehow, without precisely having planned it, he found himself taking the long way home, and somehow, he even managed to lose his way in the normally familiar streets. It was late by the time he got back to his little room.

On top of the pile of Latin books, he saw a note. He read it by the unsteady light of a fluttering candle:

They know everything. I am in tears as I write this. Father gave me a belting. It's awful. They will never let me go out alone again. You are right. We must get away. To America or wherever you want. I'll be at the station tomorrow morning early, at six o'clock. There's a train. It's the one that Father always takes when he goes hunting. I have no idea what its destination is. I must end this letter here. Someone is coming. Just be there. Without fail. Tomorrow at six.

    Yours until death,
    Anna

It was nobody, after all. Where do you think we should go? Do you have any money? I have eight gulden. I am sending this letter by our family's maid to yours. I'm not afraid of anything any more.

    I think it was your Aunt Marie who blabbed. It seems she <u>did</u> see us on Sunday.

Fritz paced up and down with long, determined strides. He felt as if he had been set free. His heart was thudding. Suddenly, he knew what it was to be a man. She trusts me! I can protect her! He was so happy.

She will be utterly mine, he thought.

And then a question occurred to him: Where to? The question began to echo round his head. Fritz drowned it out by jumping to his feet and starting to pack. He laid out some linen and a few overgarments and put what money he had saved into a black leather pouch. He was full of restless energy. Pointlessly, he threw open all his drawers and cupboards, took things out and then put them back again, threw all the books off his desk into a corner of the room, as if flamboyantly demonstrating: This is it, I'm off!

It was past midnight by the time he finally sat down on the edge of his bed. He had no thought of going to sleep. Still fully dressed, he lay down, but only because his back ached, probably from bending over so much. Again and again he asked himself: Where to? Out loud, he said: 'If we truly love each other…'

The clock ticked. In the street below, a cab rumbled by, making the window panes rattle. The clock, apparently still exhausted after the effort of its last twelve strokes, took a deep breath and managed, 'One'. That was all it could do.

Fritz heard it striking as if from a long way off and he thought: If we…truly…

When dawn finally broke, he was sitting shivering against his pillows. What had also dawned on him was a sudden certainty: I don't love Anna any more. His head felt like lead. I don't love Anna any more. Had she really meant all this? Really meant to run away, just because she'd had a belting from her father? Where had she planned to go? Fritz racked his brains, trying to remember if she had told him. What was her plan? Somewhere—anywhere. He felt outraged. And what about me? he thought. I am supposed to leave everything behind, I suppose? My parents and—and everything? Oh, and my future too, of course. My future and everything that lies before me. How idiotic of Anna, how hateful! Had she really been serious?

It made him want to box her ears. Could she really have been serious?

When the early May sunlight came flooding into the room, it seemed so bright and cheerful that Fritz decided she couldn't have meant it seriously. He told himself to calm down and toyed with the idea of staying in bed. But then he said to himself: No, I will go to the station, just to see for myself that she isn't there. And he thought about how happy it would make him to see that Anna really wasn't there.

Shivering a little from the chill of early morning, as well as from a numb sensation of weariness in his legs, he walked towards the station building. The main concourse was deserted. Half-anxious, half-hopeful, he looked about him.

No light brown jacket.

Fritz breathed a sigh of relief. He walked along all the side corridors and into all the ticket halls. Travellers were wandering up and down, still half asleep; porters were lounging against tall pillars and clusters of people with third-class tickets sat glumly on dusty window sills, surrounded by bundles and baskets.

No light brown jacket.

In one of the waiting-rooms, the announcer called out a string of destinations. He rang a shrill bell, then called out the same string of destinations somewhere very close to Fritz's ear; and then a third time, on the platform. And every time, the ugly bell sounded. Fritz turned and took himself back to the main concourse, his hands dug deep into his trouser pockets. He was entirely satisfied and thought to himself, with a little air of triumph: No light brown jacket. I knew it.

And then, perhaps a little too confident, he stepped behind a pillar. He wanted to look at the timetable, to see where this fateful six o'clock train would actually have taken him. And as his eyes travelled down the list of stations, his face took on the expression of a person standing at the top of a crooked flight of stairs down which, in the nick of time, he has saved himself from tumbling headlong.

And then he heard the patter of hurrying footsteps on the flagstones. He looked up to see a small figure at the entrance to the platforms. A figure in a light brown jacket and a hat with a bobbing rose.

Fritz just stared.

And suddenly he was gripped by a terror of this pale, fragile girl, a girl who could just play with life like this. And as if he feared she might come and find him and force him to go with her into that peculiar, unknown world, he gathered his wits, and turned and ran as fast as he could, without looking round, back towards the city.

Die Flucht. 1896/7

Arthur Schnitzler

THE GREEK DANCER

People can say what they like, but I don't believe that Mathilde Samodeski died of a heart attack. I know better than that. I don't plan to go to the house from which she is being taken today, to her longed-for rest; I have no desire to see the man who knows as well as I do why she died, to shake him by the hand and say nothing.

I choose a different destination; it is slightly further away, but it is a lovely, peaceful autumn day and it feels good to be alone. Soon I will be standing behind the garden gate where I saw Mathilde for the last time, in spring. The shutters will be closed over all the villa's windows, the gravel walks will be strewn with autumn leaves, but at a certain point, shimmering through the branches, I will probably glimpse the white marble of the *Greek Dancer*.

I find myself thinking back to that evening quite often. It seems almost a force of happenstance that made me decide, at the very last minute, to accept the Wartenheimers' invitation, since over the years I have lost my love of crowds. Perhaps it was the fault of the mild evening breeze, which blew into town from the hills and lured me out to the countryside. Because after all, it was to be a garden party, a house-warming affair for the Wartenheimers' new villa; there was no reason to fear any particular obligation. It is also strange that, as I was making my way out there, the possibility of seeing Mathilde scarcely occurred to me. And yet I was fully aware that Wartenheimer had bought the *Greek Dancer* for his villa from Samodeski—and that Mrs Wartenheimer, along with every single other woman, was in love with the sculptor; I knew that full well. But quite apart from all this, there were plenty of other reasons why I might have thought of Mathilde, for I had spent many a pleasant hour with her when she was still an unmarried girl. In particular, there was a summer on Lake Geneva, seven years ago, just a year before she got engaged. It was a summer I shall not easily forget. It seems that, in spite of my grey hair, I had allowed my ideas to carry me away, for when she became Samodeski's wife the following year, I felt a stab of disappointment and was completely certain—or rather, even hoped—that she could never be happy with him. The next time I saw Mathilde was at the reception that Gregor Samodeski gave in his studio in the Gußhausgasse, shortly after their return from honeymoon; it was a party where all the guests had preposterously been asked to come in Chinese or Japanese costume. Mathilde greeted me quite naturally; her whole manner gave an impression of easy contentment. But later, while she was talking to other people, I found myself noticing a strange look in her eyes, and after considering it for a while, I realised that I knew what it meant. 'Dear friend,' it said, 'you think he married me for my money; you think he doesn't love me; you think I am unhappy—but you are mistaken. You are completely mistaken. See how cheerful I am, how my eyes shine?

I saw her a few more times after that, but only very briefly. Once, on a journey, our trains crossed; I dined with her and her husband in a station restaurant and he told all sorts of jokes that I didn't find funny. I also spoke to her once at the theatre; she had gone with her mother, who I had to admit was still more beautiful than her daughter. God knows where Mr Samodeski was on that occasion. And last winter I saw her in the Prater; on a clear, cold day. She was walking across the snow with her little girl, under the bare chestnut trees. Their carriage followed slowly behind them. I was on the other side of the road and did not even bother to cross over. I was probably preoccupied by other things; and in any case, I was no longer particularly interested in Mathilde by that stage. So perhaps I would not be thinking about her and her sudden death today if it hadn't been for that last encounter at the Wartenheimers' villa.

I remember the evening now with a peculiar, almost painful, clarity; the way I still remember some of those days on Lake Geneva. Dusk was already falling by the time I arrived. The guests were strolling along the gravel walks. I exchanged greetings with the host and with a couple of old acquaintances. From somewhere came the sound of a small orchestra hidden in the bushes. I soon reached the little pond, surrounded by a hemicycle of tall trees; and in the centre of it, on a dark pedestal that made her seem to float above the water, shone the *Greek Dancer*, somewhat theatrically illuminated by electric light from the house. I remember the sensation that that sculpture had caused at the Secession[1] the year before; I must confess that it made an impression on me, too, although I dislike Samodeski intensely. But I have the strange feeling that it is not really he who creates the beautiful things he sometimes succeeds in creating; it is something else, something intangible and incandescent; something demonic, if you like, a flame which will certainly sputter out when he ceases to be young and lionised. I think the same is true of a great many artists and it is a fact that has always filled me with a certain satisfaction.

It was near the pond that I met Mathilde. She was walking on the arm of a young man who looked like a member of a student fraternity and who introduced himself to me as a relation of the hosts. Chatting amicably, the three of us walked up and down the garden, where lanterns were now shimmering everywhere. Our hostess came up to us with Samodeski. We all stopped for a while and, to my own amazement, I heard myself make some complimentary remarks to the sculptor about the *Greek Dancer*. It was not entirely my fault: there seemed to be a kind of benevolence in the air, as sometimes happens on such spring evenings. People who are normally indifferent to each other exchange exuberant greetings; and those already linked by a certain bond of sympathy feel compelled to display all manner of fulsome sentiment. A little while later, for example, as I sat on a bench smoking a cigarette, I was joined by a gentleman whom I knew only superficially and who suddenly began to speak highly of people like our host, people who make such noble use of their wealth. I agreed with him wholeheartedly, although I usually consider Mr Wartenheimer to be a weak-minded snob. And then, again without any reason, I went on to share with him my views on modern sculpture, a subject I know very little about; my views would ordinarily have been of no interest to him whatsoever; but under the influence of the seductive spring evening, he agreed with me enthusiastically. Later, I ran into our host's nieces, who were finding the party unutterably romantic, mainly because there were lanterns flickering amongst the leaves and because, so they said, there was music playing 'somewhere in the distance'. We were standing right next to the orchestra at the time, but I still didn't find their remark idiotic. That's how far I had fallen under the spell of the prevailing mood.

Dinner was served at small tables which were set up on the wide terrace, as far as space allowed, and partly also in the adjoining salon. The three large glass doors stood wide. I was seated at an outside table with one of the nieces; on my other side sat Mathilde with the young man who looked like a fraternity student but who turned out to be a bank clerk and reserve officer. Opposite us, at a table in the salon, sat Samodeski, between our hostess and a beautiful lady I did not know. He blew his wife a jocularly flamboyant kiss; she nodded to him and smiled. Without meaning to, I found myself watching him rather closely. He really was extremely good-looking, with his steel-blue eyes and his tapering black beard, which he stroked from time to time with two fingers of his left hand. I do not think I have ever in my life seen a man enwrapped in such a glowing nimbus of words, looks and gestures as Samodeski was that evening. At first, it seemed as if he was just allowing it to happen. But I soon saw, from his way of whispering surreptitiously to the women, from his loathsome expression of triumph and especially from the tense excitement of the women on either side of him, that their seemingly harmless conversation was being stoked by some illicit fire.

Of course, Mathilde must have seen all this just as well as I did; but she went on chatting, apparently unmoved, sometimes to her neighbour, sometimes to me. After a while, she turned her attention solely to me, enquired about one or two general things and asked me to tell her about my trip to Athens the previous year. Then she talked about her little girl, who already had the remarkable ability to pick up Schumann *Lieder* by ear. She told me that her parents had bought a little house in Hietzing, for their old age. She mentioned some altar cloths and other old church textiles that she had acquired in Salzburg the previous year; she went on to talk about a hundred other things. But beneath the surface, something quite different was going on between us; a silent, bitter battle was being waged: she was trying, with her tranquil demeanour, to convince me that her happiness was complete—and I refused to believe her. Once again, I remembered that Chinese-Japanese evening in Samodeski's studio, where she had done the same thing. Tonight, she could sense that she was doing little to allay my fears and that she would have to come up with something very special to dispel them.

And that is what gave her the idea of drawing my attention to the eager, besotted way the two beautiful ladies were fawning on her husband. She began to speak of the easy way he had with women, as if she could glory in it as a faithful companion, without any misgivings or mistrust, just as she also gloried in his good looks and his artistic genius. But the harder she tried to seem cheerful and calm, the deeper the shadows that fell across her brow. Once, when she raised her glass to Samodeski, I saw that her hand shook. She tried to conceal it, to suppress it; but this caused not only her hand, but also her arm and her whole body to become so rigid for a few moments that I was almost afraid. She regained her composure, threw me a quick, sidelong glance, evidently saw that she was on the point of losing the battle, and suddenly said, as if making a last, desperate *sortie*:

'I expect you think I'm jealous.' And before I had time to reply, she went on, 'Oh, plenty of people think that. To begin with, Gregor thought so, too.' She spoke deliberately loudly; the people at her husband's table could easily have heard every word. 'Well,' she said, glancing over at them, 'when one is married to a man like that, so handsome and famous— and when one has a reputation for not being particularly handsome oneself… Oh, you don't have to say anything. Though I know I'm bit prettier since I had my little girl…'

She was probably right, but to her husband—I was quite convinced of this—the nobility of her features had never meant a great deal, and as far as her figure was concerned, she had probably lost the only charm she ever had for him with the departure of her girlish slenderness. But I agreed with her, of course; I fell over myself to do so.

She seemed pleased, for she went on, with growing good humour: 'But I haven't the least talent for jealousy. I wasn't aware of it at first; I only realised it gradually, and then very definitely a few years ago, in Paris. You knew that we were there, didn't you?'

Yes, I remembered.

'Gregor sculpted the busts of Princesse La Hire and Minister Chocquet there, along with a lot of other things. We led such a pleasant life in Paris, as young people… I mean, we still *are* young, of course, but there we lived like lovers, though we did occasionally go out into the wider world as well. We went to the Austrian Ambassador's a few times, and we visited the La Hires and others. But on the whole, we didn't care much for society. We even lived all the way out in Montmartre, in a really rather shabby house, where Gregor also had his studio. Some of the young artists we knew had absolutely no idea we were married. I went everywhere with Gregor. I spent long nights with him in the Café d'Athènes, with Léandre, Carabin and people like that. All sorts of women belonged to our circle, women I probably wouldn't want to associate with in Vienna—although after all…' She cast a furtive glance at Mrs Wartenheimer and then went on, 'And some of them were very pretty. Henri Chabran's last mistress was there a couple of times, the woman who after his death wore nothing but black and had a different lover every week but insisted they all observe mourning, too… One meets such odd people. And as you can imagine, there were women chasing after my husband no less madly there than anywhere else; it was enough to make one laugh. But as I was always with him—or mostly, anyway—they didn't dare approach him, particularly since everyone assumed I was his mistress. Oh, to think if they had known that I was merely his wife!

And then I came up with a quaint idea that you would never have believed me capable of—to be honest, I'm still amazed at my own daring…' She stared straight ahead, speaking more quietly than before: 'It's also possible, by the way, that it had something to do with—well, you can imagine. I had known for a few weeks that I was expecting a baby. It made me terribly happy. At the beginning I was not only more cheerful, but strangely enough I seemed much more—well, flexible than before… Anyway, one lovely spring evening, I dressed up like a man and went off on an adventure with Gregor. Of course, I made him promise that he wouldn't do anything he wouldn't normally do—otherwise there would have been no point to the whole thing. I looked superb, by the way; you would never have recognised me. Nobody would have recognised me. A friend of Gregor's, a certain Léonce Albert, a young painter, a hunchback, came to fetch us. It was lovely weather, May, very warm—and I was ever so brazen… Don't get the wrong idea, but I took off my overcoat—a very elegant yellow overcoat, it was—and just slung it over my arm, the way gentlemen do. Can you imagine? But it was already quite dark by then. We had dinner in a small restaurant on the outer Boulevard, then we went to the Roulotte, where Legay was singing and Montoya… "*Tu t'en iras les pieds devant…*" You heard that here recently, didn't you? At the Wiednertheater.'

At this point Mathilde glanced over at her husband, but he wasn't paying any attention to her. It was as if she was bidding him a long farewell. And then she went back to her story, her voice getting more and more vehement, as if hurrying it on.

'In the Roulotte,' she said, 'there was a very elegant

woman sitting quite close to us; she was flirting with Gregor, but in such a way... Well, I mean, you never saw anything more indecent. I couldn't understand why her husband didn't throttle her on the spot. *I* would have done. I think she was a duchess... Well, you needn't laugh, she was definitely someone from the *beau monde*, despite her behaviour. And I actually wanted Gregor to go along with it—of course I did! I would like to have seen how one begins a thing like that. I should like to have seen him slip her a note, or do something else, the sort of thing he would have done in such a situation before I married him. Yes, I really wanted that, although it would not have been without a certain risk for him. We women seem to be afflicted by such gruesome curiosity. But luckily, Gregor wasn't in the mood. And then, not long afterwards, we left. We went back out into the beautiful May night. Léonce was still with us. In fact, he fell in love with me that night and, contrary to his usual behaviour, became positively gallant. He was normally so shy, you see—because of his appearance. "It takes a yellow overcoat to make one set one's cap at someone," I said. And on we went, as merrily as a trio of students. And now comes the interesting part: we went to the Moulin Rouge. It was always part of the plan. It was also time for something finally to happen. Up until then, there had been nothing at all. The only incident was when I was accosted in the street. Yes, I was the one who was accosted, if you can believe it—by a woman! That had certainly not been part of my intention. At around one o'clock, we got to the Moulin Rouge. You probably know what goes on there; I had actually imagined it would be worse. To begin with, nothing happened at all and it looked as if the whole joke was going to fall flat. I was a bit annoyed about it. "You're such a child," Gregor said. "What did you expect? That we'd get here and women would instantly start flinging themselves at our feet?" He said "our feet" out of politeness to Léonce, though of course there was no question of anyone flinging themselves at Léonce's feet. But then, just as we were all seriously thinking of going home, things took a turn. I noticed someone—and yes, *I* was the one who noticed her—a woman who had happened to go past us a few times. She was very serious and looked rather different from most of the other women there. Her clothes weren't remotely showy; she was dressed completely in white. I had noticed how she had given no encouragement at all to the two or three gentlemen who approached her; she just walked on without sparing them a glance. She kept her eyes on the dancing, very calm, very intent; very objective, one might say. Léonce asked a few people if they had ever seen the pretty little thing before—I had asked him to do this—and one man remembered having seen her the previous winter at one of the Thursday dances in the Latin Quarter. Léonce then went over to speak to her, and she consented to speak to him, too. Then he brought her back to join us and we all went and sat down at a little table and drank champagne. Gregor didn't pay her the least attention—she might just as well not have been there. He carried on chatting to me, only ever to me. And that seemed somehow to encourage her. She became more and more cheerful, more talkative, more uninhibited, and by the end she had practically told us her whole life story. What things a poor creature like that experiences—or perhaps is forced to experience! One reads about this sort of thing so often, of course, but when one actually hears it as something real, from someone sitting right next to you, it's very strange. I still remember quite a lot of it. When she was fifteen, she was seduced and abandoned. Then she worked as a model and as an extra in a small theatre. The things she told us about the director of that theatre! I would have got up and left if I hadn't been a little tipsy from the champagne. Then she fell in love with a medical student who worked in the anatomy faculty and whom she sometimes went to meet at the morgue—or rather, she didn't just meet him there; I mean, they... No, I can't possibly repeat some of the things she told us! The medical student left her too, of course. And she didn't want to go on living after that, so she killed herself—or at least, she tried to. She made light of it all in the way she told it. I can still hear her voice. She made it all seem far less awful than it was. And then she pulled back her dress a little and showed us a small, reddish scar above her left breast. And as we were all looking at it, very intently, she suddenly said—no, she *shouted* at my husband: "Kiss my scar!" Well, as I've told you, Gregor wasn't paying the smallest attention to her. Even while she was telling her stories, he hardly listened, just looked around the room, smoking. So when she appealed to him like that, he barely smiled. But I prodded him, I pinched him—I was really a bit befuddled by the champagne; at any rate, I was in the strangest mood I've ever been in in my life. And whether Gregor wanted to or not, he had to—well, he had to at least pretend to touch the scar with his lips. Oh, and then things got funnier than ever. I've never laughed as much as I did that evening, though without ever really knowing what at. And I would never have thought it possible that a woman—a woman like her—could fall so desperately in love with someone in the course of a single hour as this creature did with Gregor. Her name was Madeleine.'

I don't know whether Mathilde pronounced the name louder on purpose; at any rate, it seemed to me that her husband heard it, for he looked over at us, although strangely enough, he didn't look at his wife, but his eyes met mine and we stared at each other for quite a while, placidly enough, though not notably sympathetically. Then, suddenly, he smiled at his wife. She nodded in return, and then he turned back to his neighbours and she turned back to me.

'Of course I can't remember everything Madeleine said after that,' she said. 'It had all become such a whirl. But I'll admit, there was a moment when I got a little upset. It was when Madeleine seized my husband's hand and kissed it. It was all over in an instant but at that moment, you see, I thought of our child. And I felt how indissolubly linked Gregor and I had become, and how everything else was just insubstantial semblance—mere fancy, just play-acting, like that night. And then suddenly, everything was all right again. We all went and sat in a coffee house on the Boulevard until dawn. And then I heard Madeleine ask my husband to see her home. He just laughed at her. But then, to bring the fun to a happy and, in a way, advantageous end—you know what egotists all artists are, at least as far as their art is concerned… Well, he told her that he was a sculptor and suggested she might come to his studio, because he wanted to sculpt her. And she said: 'If you're a sculptor, I'll eat my hat! But I'll come.'

Mathilde fell silent. But I have never seen a woman's eyes express—or conceal—so much suffering. And then at last she composed herself for the final thing she wanted to say, and she went on with her story.

'Gregor was adamant that I should be in the studio the next day. He even suggested that I stay hidden behind the curtain when Madeleine came. Well, I know there are plenty of women who would have gone along with it. But I think, either one trusts or one doesn't. And I have chosen to trust. Am I not right to do so?' She turned wide, interrogative eyes on me.

I just nodded, and she went on, 'Madeleine came the next day, of course. And after that she came very often… Like all the others before and after her. And you can take it from me that she was one of the most beautiful. After all, you yourself stood admiring her only today, over there by the pond.'

'The *Greek Dancer*?'

'Yes. Madeleine was his model for it. And yet you imagine I was suspicious—of her and all the others! But wouldn't I just have made his life and mine a misery by being suspicious? I am very glad that I have no talent for jealousy.'

Someone was standing in the wide central doorway and had started to make what was probably a very droll toast to our host, because people were laughing heartily. I looked at Mathilde, but she wasn't listening to it any more than I was. And I saw how she looked over at her husband and gave him a look that not only betrayed an undying love, but also feigned an unshakeable confidence, as if it were her sacred duty not to hinder in any way his enjoyment of his own existence. And he received that look complacently and unabashed—although of course he knew as well as I did that she was suffering, and had suffered like a beast all her life.

And that is why I don't believe the story of the heart attack. I got to know Mathilde too well that evening, and for me it is all completely clear. Just as, from the first moment to the last, she played the part of happy wife, for the benefit of her husband, while he lied to her and drove her mad, so she finally staged a natural death, when in fact she threw her own life away because she could not bear it any longer. And he accepted this final sacrifice from her, completely as if it were his due.

So here I stand in front of the railings. The shutters are firmly closed. The little villa stands white and as if enchanted in the twilight, and the marble dancer shimmers between the autumn branches.

Perhaps I am being unfair to Samodeski, by the way. It might be that ultimately he is so stupid that he really hasn't divined the truth. But it saddens me to think that in death there could be no greater joy for Mathilde than to know that her last devoted deception had succeeded.

Or am I completely wrong? Was it a natural death after all? No. I will not deprive myself of the right to hate the man Mathilde loved so much. It will probably be my only pleasure for some time to come…

Die griechische Tänzerin. 1902

Egid Filek von Wittinghausen
THE GLASS DOOR

He comes home late again. With red-rimmed eyes and a glassy, mulish look. Then a coarse, rasping laugh and a thump of his clenched fist on the table, where the bottle stands next to the smouldering tallow candle. After that, he turns his fist on Mother, before dropping like a stone onto the filthy bed.

Mother crawls out of her corner and sets to snivelling and scolding by turns. Firstly at herself and her wretched life with this brute of a husband, who earns so little and yet fritters away what *kreuzers* he has on *schnaps*; and then at her daughter, who sits at the table with her head propped on her thin, still-childlike arms. She will be turned out of the house if she doesn't start bringing in more money than that miserable pittance of a factory wage. How much longer does she expect to be fed? She is already past fifteen…

The girl just sits with her face turned away, staring blankly in front of her, as if none of it were any of her business. She knows what's coming. Mother will continue to scold and sniff for another quarter of an hour. Then Father will start snoring and Mother will throw herself down on the rumpled bed and weep. Her sobs will gradually get quieter. And then everything in the stuffy room will subside into silence. And tomorrow it will all begin again, just the same as today…

For half an hour longer the young girl sits there without moving, staring into the candle flame. Then she lifts her head and looks over at her parents. Neither of them is awake any longer. Her father moans in his sleep, her mother's hand hangs limply over the edge of the bed. The girl takes a deep breath, brushes the hair from her forehead and reaches for the long grey shawl hanging over the back of the chair.

Out into the fresh air; just for half an hour. Tomorrow at peep of day she has to go to work again, amid the smoke and the fumes of the booming machine room. And she feels so unwell, her eyes are dizzy and her ears are a-buzz. She gets that dizzy feeling so often now; it has been like this for about six months. The fresh air will make her feel better.

Slowly, very slowly, she turns the doorknob and slips outside. She creeps down the dark wooden stairs, past the life-size wooden statue of Christ and the little red lamp that burns in front of it. Then she steals across the cold stone flags. As she pulls opens the heavy front door, the draught puts out the flickering eternal flame.

Outside, the winter night is clear and moonlit. She pulls her shawl tighter and wanders slowly through the lonely, echoing streets; past a row of low windows curtained in dark red, behind which wild singing and carousing can be heard; past large, high, round-arched windows whose white, silent curtains shimmer in the cold moonlight. Up there, behind the lone window where a light still dimly burns, lies the old grandee, the factory owner for whom she works. He has been bed-ridden for some time: incurable, the doctors say. She scuttles quickly past, glad to be young and healthy. The earlier dizzy feeling has gone; deeply and greedily, she sucks in the cold, fresh air. The city's bell-towers strike the hour but she doesn't notice how time flies by; instead she keeps on walking, further and further…

She turns into the main street. The Auer lamps[2] cast their greenish glow in a long double string. The tram tracks gleam in the cold moonlight, stretching away until they merge into a flickering dot in the distance. She feels tempted to let her footsteps follow where they lead—slow and regular all night long, and throughout the day that follows, on and on…

The tracks lead to a large square planted with trees, with snow-covered flowerbeds and narrow gravel walks and a bronze monument, rearing black and dark into the night sky from a circular patch of grass in the middle. The man on the plinth is cloaked in snow; a crown of ice surmounts his head; and his hand, outstretched in a gesture of command, is similarly burdened with white. The square is surrounded by tall trees thick with snow, awkwardly lifting their branches towards the sky. Beneath them, a soft white carpet covers everything, smooths everything out, even swallows the sound of the girl's light footsteps. It seems such a secret, intimate world; she half-expects someone to take her hand and whisper softly: 'Come with me!'

Behind the monument, a large and magnificent house stands silhouetted against the sky, a house with turrets and pointed gables and brightly-lit arched windows. And suddenly, she hears muffled sounds emerging from the silence: dance music. She listens. There is a ball being held in that magnificent house tonight. If only she could see what a grand ballroom looks like, what the ladies are wearing and how well-to-do people converse! She creeps around the house to the side entrance with its carpeted stairway. The door stands open. There is no one there. Slowly, she climbs the steps, stopping to listen after each one.

The sound of waltz music gets closer and closer. And suddenly she finds herself in front of a large glass door leading into the anteroom. The music falls silent. She presses her face against the glass and peers into the room.

The musicians are having a break. Double doors stand open to right and left, and laughing, chattering couples are streaming into the cool anteroom. More and more people come; they all walk past the glass door, behind which the girl stands with her face pressed against the glass. Most of them barely register her presence; some crowd around the buffet, others begin flocking into the large dining-room, others sit down on the dark red couches grouped around the palm-fringed rondeau and listlessly fan themselves with their silk stoles. The palm tree leaves waft slowly up and down; everything shimmers and glitters in the glow of the myriad electric lights, lights that are reflected in the polished parquet floor. In they come, all those important, well-to-do people, people to whom she must offer the sacrifice of her young life.

But there is no place in her heart for such bitter thoughts tonight. She gazes at the splendour with wide, shining eyes. What a magnificent pearl necklace that young lady is wearing! And in her ears hang diamonds, big and shining! Oh, what this girl would give to have one—just one—of those sparkling brilliants! Then she would be free, she could live by herself and no longer have to put up with her father's boorishness and her mother's whines.

The young lady is talking to a gentleman now—he turns from her with a bow. It's the son of the factory owner himself. He stands in a corner, surveying all the women and young girls, appraising them with the same dispassionate, assessing expression she saw in his eyes this morning, when he examined the cloth in the cutting room, pulling out each bolt of fabric one by one. A couple of older ladies have gone to sit on a red couch; they look so tired, so done-in; they are checking their watches. How weary they seem—in the midst of so much light and colour and beauty…

Another young man comes to lean against the glass door. He peels off a white glove, lights a slim cigar and idly regards the rings of smoke that slowly float upward in coils and tendrils, in quickly dissipating, blue-grey spirals. He looks over the heads of all the people, looks up at the ceiling and gnaws at his lower lip. A stale, jumbled scent of erotic perfume, of tobacco, of heady hothouse flowers and heated young human bodies hangs over the whole room. Two prominent businessmen are standing by the green-leather palm trees. They are talking about their weaving yarn, assessing its chances of success, complaining about the inferior quality of Australian wool.

A hopeful young civil servant is now walking on the arm of the beautiful lady with the pearl necklace; the lady is his employer's wife and the young man wants to make a name for himself—the whole town knows that. A little further away, the old magnate himself stands yawning superciliously while a bevy of bank clerks make themselves agreeable to his daughters. In the dining-room next door, champagne corks are popping. Some show-off wants the world to see how wealthy he is. From a phalanx of cigarettes, thin trails of smoke drift up to the ceiling, casting a blue veil across the faces of the ladies on the red couch. When their conversation lags for a moment and their faces fall into repose, there are large, bluish circles around their eyes, like on the faces of exhausted actors struggling to keep going to the end of the play. And in the midst of all the weary hustle and bustle, there go the giddy little debutantes, eagerly drinking in their very first ball, with wide, eager eyes and radiant delight on their sweet, silly faces.

Where is the fair-haired girl he came here for today? The young man leaning on the glass door searches for her with his eyes. Ah—there she is, over there by the curtains, with her mother by her side. She is being given a lecture on what is and isn't 'done'. She has 'compromised' herself. Her little blonde head begins to droop; her cheeks turn red; her white-gloved fingers mechanically fold and unfold a corner of her dance card. She is a good girl; she will do just as Mamma tells her; never again will she sit with him in the gallery during the quadrille, and chatter as merrily as she did just now; instead, she will dance very sedately and properly, be polite to all the young men, learn the same gracious, social smile as the one affected by her mother, until the realms of decorum and indecency are divided for her once and for all by an iron partition. He smiles bitterly. Another example of the grotesque perjury of life that all of these people perpetrate and which he—mercilessly and at the expense of all his illusions—detects in them now with such savage glee. He is fully aware of not being one iota better than they are; he knows that his own subterfuges are perhaps even more grotesque than those of all the others. And the cruellest thing is, that these falsehoods are as necessary as truth itself, because they hold the world together, like a rusty set of clamps that threatens to splinter the overburdened picture rail it supports, but which one can never remove, because otherwise the house would collapse in ruins.

Suddenly, he hears a little sigh behind him. Astonished, he turns round. There stands a little working girl, a girl whose cheeks are red with the cold, whose clammy mouth hangs half-open with yearning. Her grey woollen shawl has slipped from her head, revealing straw-blonde hair wound over her low forehead in meagre plaits. Her bright blue eyes gaze longingly into the hall, as if peering through a gap in the trees into a Garden of Eden. At the sight of her, the cold, stiff society mask falls from the young man's face and he smiles—a half-amused, half-pitying smile—at the little thing on the far side of the door.

The girl can feel his eyes upon her. And suddenly, her thin face is suffused by a rosy glow. A ray from a foreign world has struck her, a ray of warmth from that shining, fragrant, blissful realm beyond the glass door… She hears the approach of stern, heavy footsteps. A footman in dark blue livery, dark blue with a silver trim, steps out of a side door and walks towards her with a scowl. Quickly she turns, and scuttles down the stairs.

But the look that she felt upon her then, that silent, warm, benevolent look, stays with her. She takes it out into the glittering winter moonlit night, back to the barren desolation of her parents' home.

Die Glastür. 1903

Stefan Zweig

THE STAR ABOVE THE TREES

François, the waiter, was serving dinner. Slim and impeccably groomed, he leaned forward over the shoulder of the lovely Polish Countess Ostrowska; and as he did so, something strange happened. It only lasted for a second and it was not that he winced or started; there was no movement, no reaction involved. And yet it was one of those moments in which thousands of hours and days of ecstasy and agony are condensed, just as the untamed might of the great, dark rustling oak trees with their swaying branches and tossing leaves is distilled in a single dusty scattering of seed. No, nothing outward occurred. François, the dapper waiter at the grand Riviera hotel, merely bent lower to set the platter more directly in the path of the Countess's questing knife and fork. And in doing so, his face hovered momentarily above the softly curled, fragrant billow of her hair; and as he instinctively raised his deferentially lowered lids, his gaze became dizzily aware of how gracefully her white neck curved away and was lost in the dark red folds of her gown. Awareness flared up inside him with a phosphor glow. And her knife clinked softly against his imperceptibly trembling platter. Yet although he sensed at once the perilous consequences of this sudden enchantment, he deftly mastered his agitation and continued to serve with the cool and faintly gallant aplomb of the discreet flunkey that he was. He calmly offered the platter to the Countess's habitual dining companion, an elderly, elegantly graceful aristocrat who conversed on neutral topics with a subtle intonation and in crystalline French. Then he retired from the table without a gesture or a glance.

Those moments were the beginning of a strange, devoted sense of being lost, a feeling so heady and drunken that the proud and weighty word 'love' became it singularly ill. This was a canine, faithful kind of love, a love unallied to desire, a love which people hardly ever feel in the full flush of their maturity. It is only the very young and the very old who can love in such a way. It is a love which does not calculate or think; it only dreams. François completely forgot the undeserved yet undeniable condescension which even clever and considerate people show towards those in waiter's garb; he did not ponder possibilities and eventualities but instead allowed this strange feeling to course through his veins until its secret intimacy went beyond the reach of mockery or censure. This was no lewd fancy fed by winks and surreptitious nudges; no suddenly staked claim attended by flamboyant gesticulation; no ardour of pining lips and quivering hands. No, it was a quiet devotion; fulfilled through a performance of those small services which are all the more sublime in their humility because they remain knowingly unnoticed. When dinner was over, he smoothed the wrinkles in the tablecloth in front of where she had sat with a touch as tender and as that with which one strokes one's beloved's hands; he arranged the things beside her place with devoted symmetry, as if readying them for a feast.

Carefully, he bore the glasses that her lips had touched to his cramped and dingy attic room and there he let them sparkle, like precious jewels in the pearly moonlight. From every corner where he found himself on duty, attendant yet apart, he secretly observed her every step. When she spoke, he drank it in as one would savour a sweet and perfumed wine, eagerly seizing each sentence, each command, like a child catching a flying ball. Thus his besotted soul bestowed a rich and ever-changing radiance upon the meagre monotony of his life. He never committed the sober folly of cloaking the whole thing in the cold, annihilating language of fact. To wit: François, a humble waiter, loves an exotic, eternally unattainable countess. For he did not consider her as real; instead, he thought of her as something very remote and distant, touching life with nothing more than a reflective glow. He loved the imperious arrogance of her commands, the proud arc of her black eyebrows, the way they almost met in the middle; and the savage crease beside her narrow lips, the confident grace of her gestures. Submissiveness seemed to him to come as a matter of course; the lowly services he was called upon to perform did not confer humiliation but instead the joy of being so often allowed to enter the magical circle that surrounded her.

And thus, in the life of this modest man, a fantasy unfurled, like a noble and carefully cultivated garden flower that blooms beside a road where other seedlings stifle in the dust. His was the giddiness of a simple person for whom an enchanted, intoxicating dream has taken flesh in the midst of a dreary, humdrum life. But the dreams of such people are like rudderless ships that aimlessly drift and toss upon mirror-like waters until, with a sudden jolt, their keels run aground on an unknown shore.

And reality is stronger and more robust than dreams. One evening, the fat doorman from the Canton de Vaud remarked in passing: 'Madame Ostrowska is leaving tomorrow on the eight o'clock train.' Then came a few more names that meant nothing and which François scarcely heard. Because the news had set off a confused roaring and whirling in his head. More than once, he ran his fingers over his aching brow, as if to peel away an oppressive film that lay across it, dulling his understanding. He took a few steps; it was more like a stagger. Bewildered and afraid, he stepped in front of a tall, gilt mirror and saw a pale, unfamiliar face staring chalkily out at him. His ideas would not form themselves; they seemed immured behind a dark wall of fog. Clinging almost unconsciously to the banister, he groped his way down the wide stairs and out into the twilit garden, where the tall pines stood lonely like dark thoughts. He swayed unsteadily forward, his steps like the low and clumsy flight of a great, dark bird of night, then sank onto a bench and leant his head against the cool backrest. It was very quiet there. Between clipped bushes, the sea sparkled, glowing with faintly trembling lights, and the sing-song murmur of the distant surf was swallowed up by the silence.

And then, suddenly, everything seemed clear, completely clear. So painfully clear that he almost smiled. It was over, that was all. Countess Ostrowska would go back home;

François the waiter would remain at his post. Was that so strange? Did not all the guests who came here go away again after two weeks, after three, after four? How foolish not to have thought of this before. It was all so clear, so clear that it made one want to laugh, to weep. He laughed out loud at the sudden stab of pain. And his thoughts whirred and whirred around his head. Tomorrow evening, on the eight o'clock train to Warsaw. To Warsaw: hours and hours through forests and valleys, over hills and mountains, across steppes and rivers, through pounding cities. Warsaw! How far away it was! He could scarcely imagine it; and yet he felt it deeply; that proud and threatening, hard and distant word: Warsaw.

And... For a second, he felt a vague fluttering of hope. He could go there too! He could hire himself out as a footman or a clerk, as a carter—as a slave. He could stand on street corners as a freezing beggar. Anything so as not to be so horribly far away from her, but to breathe the air of the same city; perhaps once or twice to see her flash by, to catch sight of her shadow, her gown, her dark hair... Impromptu reveries began flitting before his eyes. But the hour was implacable and obdurate. He saw the impossibility of it, naked and clear. He did some arithmetic: one or two hundred francs in savings at best. That was barely enough to get halfway there. And then what? As if through a torn veil, he had a vision of his life, saw how poor, how starveling, how miserable it would become. Barren, empty years as a waiter, tormented by a foolish longing; it was absurd, derisory—but it would be his future. The realisation came over him with a shudder. And suddenly, inextricably, the threads of his ideas came together. There was only one way out...

The treetops swayed softly in a barely perceptible breeze. Before him loomed the dark, black night. Confident and calm, he rose from the bench and walked across the crunching gravel, back to the grand hotel that lay sleeping in white silence. He stopped and looked up at its windows. They were in darkness, without a single glimmer of light to kindle dreamy longings. His heart beat evenly and slow, he walked like one whom nothing can delude or deceive. In his room, he threw himself listlessly on the bed and slept a dull, dreamless sleep, until woken by the dawn alarm.

The next day, his manner was one of carefully honed consideration and deliberate calm. He went about his duties with cool impassivity; his gestures seemed so unflustered and assured that no one would have suspected the grim resolve that lay behind the mask. Shortly before dinner was due to be served, he hurried with his modest savings to the finest florist's shop and bought exquisite blooms that in their many-coloured splendour seemed to him like speech: fire-red tulips like a smouldering passion; spreading white chrysanthemums conjuring pale, exotic dreams; slender orchids, the wraith-like impersonations of desire; and a few proud, beguiling roses. And then he bought a magnificent vase of shining, opalescent glass. And the few francs he had left over he gave to a beggar child, his gesture swift and carefree as he passed the urchin in the street. Then he hurried back, and with wistful solemnity set the vase of flowers before the Countess's place, which he now laid for the last time, with slow and almost self-indulgent attention.

Then came the dinner. He served it just as usual: coolly, silently and adeptly, without looking up. Only at the end did his gaze take in the whole of her proud and supple form, a gaze without end and of which she had no inkling. Never had she seemed so beautiful to him as in that last, unseeking gaze. Then, without a farewell or any other gesture, he stepped quietly away from the table and left the room. Like a guest to whom the servants bow and bend, he walked along the corridors, then down the grand front stairs and out into the street: one had the impression that he was leaving his past behind. In front of the hotel, he paused for a second, hesitant; then turned towards a path alongside gleaming villas and expansive lawns. Rapt in thought, his steps bent inexorably onward, without knowing where they were going.

Until late into the evening he continued his aimless, unconscious rambling. No longer did he ponder the past or the inevitable. No longer, even, did he toy with thoughts of death, in the way one might raise and lower a glinting revolver in one's assessing hand, contemplating one last time its baleful, yawning barrel. He had long since pronounced his sentence on himself. Only images came now, flitting like migrating swallows. At first, his early youth, until that fateful day at school, when a foolish adventure had plucked him from a seductively beckoning future and thrust him rudely into the maelstrom of the world. Then, the ceaseless journeying, the toiling for a daily wage, the ventures that failed again and again, until the great dark wave we know as Fate eventually shattered his pride and left him beached in humble servitude.

Memories whirled in a kaleidoscope, arriving at last at the tender fancies of these final days, which illuminated and once again flung wide the dark gate of reality through which he had to pass. It came to him now that he wished to die.

For a while, he pondered the many routes that lead to death, weighing up their relative agony and speed. Then suddenly, a thought flashed through his mind, a symbol culled from his gloomy musings: just as she, oblivious and ravaging, had trampled across his destiny, so was she also to pulverise his body. She herself was to do the deed. She herself was to bring her work to a conclusion. His thoughts raced ahead with eerie assurance. In less than an hour, at eight o'clock, the Express was leaving, the train that was to take her away. He would throw himself under its wheels, allow himself to be crushed by the same violent force that was snatching the woman of his dreams away. He would bleed to death beneath her feet. One after the other, these ideas besieged his mind, as if in celebration. He knew the perfect place. Further up the wooded incline, where the view of the nearby bay finally disappeared behind the rustling treetops.

He looked at his watch: the seconds and his hammering pulse were almost keeping time. He needed to set off. And all at once, his aimless steps were filled with elasticity and purpose. On he went, with the determined, unlingering stride that massacres dreams. Headlong he rushed into the twilight splendour of the southern evening, towards the place where a purple streak of sky lay bolstered between the distant wooded hills. Onward he hurried, until he came to the railway line, twin silver tracks that shone before him and lighted his way.

They led him on a winding course through deep and fragrant valleys, shrouded in veils of mist shot through with silver by the moonlight. Upwards they drew him, into the hills, from where there was a view of the distant, night-black sea, spangled with lights strung out along the shore. And finally, he came to the deep, ever-whispering forest, which buried the tracks in its sinking shadows.

It was already late by the time he reached the dark forest slope. He was almost out of breath. The trees that enveloped him were eerie and black. Only high up in their shimmering crowns was there any light to be seen, for there, a pale moon trembled in the branches, branches which sighed when the soft night air caught them in its arms. The strange calls of a distant owl pierced the dim silence. His thoughts stood still in anxious loneliness. All he could do was wait; wait and watch for the red light of the train appearing round the first bend as the railway wound uphill. Again and once again he looked at his watch and nervously counted the seconds. Then he held his breath and listened for the distant whistle of the locomotive. Nothing. The night was completely silent once again. Time seemed to have stood still.

And then at last he saw a light, shining somewhere far below. His heart gave a lurch—whether from fear or elation he did not know. Swift and decisive, he threw himself across the tracks. At first, he only felt the momentary welcome coolness of the iron rails against his temples. Then he listened. The train was still a long way off. It might be minutes away. The only sound was the whispering wind in the trees. His thoughts danced as if on strings, until suddenly an idea landed, heavy and still, piercing his heart with a bolt of pain: he was dying for her sake and she would never know it. Not the smallest ripple from the ocean of his life had ever so much as touched her own. She would never know how another's destiny had clung to hers and been shattered by it.

Through a still night that seemed to hold its breath, the rhythmic wheezing of the approaching train surged nearer out of the distance. That last thought burned unabated in his doomed mind, tormenting his last minutes. Slowly, the train came closer and closer. He opened his eyes once more. Above him was a silent, blue-black sky and a group of rustling treetops. And high above them, a white, twinkling star. A lonely star above the trees…

The railway tracks beneath his head began to shiver and hum. But still that one idea burned in his heart and in his eyes, eyes filled with all the ardour and desperation of his love. All his longing and this last, agonised desire flowed up into the bright white star that shone so gently down on him. Nearer and nearer came the train. And once again, with one last inexpressible look, the doomed man communed with the twinkling star, the star above the trees. Then he closed his eyes. The rails shivered and heaved, the rumbling bulk of the speeding train came closer and closer so that the forest thundered as if with a peal of hammering bells. The earth seemed to reel. Another deafening hiss and a whoosh, a swirling roar, then a piercing whistle, a fearful, animal screech, the shrill protesting of inadequate brakes…

The beautiful Countess Ostrowska had her own private compartment in the train. Since her departure, she had been reading a French novel, cradled by the gentle rocking motion as the train rattled along. The air in the narrow carriage was stuffy, filled with the oppressive scent of wilting flowers. White sprays of lilac were already drooping wearily in the magnificent farewell bouquets; like overripe fruit, the blooms clung limply to their stems, and the plump and heavy rose petals seemed to shrivel in a cloud of heady fragrances. Thick, scented gusts of suffocating sultriness seemed to hang in an indolent pall, despite the restless onward racing of the train.

Suddenly, wearily, she put her book down. She could not have said exactly why. A strange sensation seemed to bore into her; an acute shaft of pain; a sharp, uncomfortable pressure round her heart. She thought she would suffocate in the sweaty, numbing fug of all the flowers. And the stabbing pain would not recede, she felt every judder of the whirring wheels, the sense of inexorable forward motion tortured her unbearably. She felt gripped by a sudden mad desire to stop the train, to wrench it back from the black hole towards which it was hurtling. Never in her life had she felt such fear, a fear of something terrible, invisible, cruel, of something clutching at her heart. In a few brief seconds, she was gripped by an incomprehensible pain, an unfathomable fear. And the feeling grew stronger and stronger, the pressure on her throat felt tighter and tighter. Like a prayer, she offered up the thought that if only the train would stop…

Then suddenly came a shrill whistle; then the protesting shriek of the locomotive and the grinding groan of the brakes.

And the rhythm of the wheels grew slower and slower, became a rattling stutter, then came to a halt with a bump…

Groggily, she groped her way to the window to drink in the cool air. The window slithered down. Outside, she saw black shapes rushing hither and thither… Words ricocheted from alternating voices. A suicide… Under the wheels… Dead… Out here in the middle of nowhere…

She shrank back. Instinctively, she lifted her eyes to the silent sky and the black, rustling forest. And higher still, to that single star above the treetops. She felt its gaze like a glistening tear. She stared up at it, and was suddenly suffused with a sadness such as she had never known. A sadness full of ardour and longing, the like of which her life had never seen…

Slowly, the train rumbles on its way. The Countess huddles in a corner as the tears begin coursing down her cheeks. The dull fear has receded; she only feels a deep and nameless pain, the source of which she ponders futilely. It is the kind of pain that frightened children feel when they wake in the depths of night and suddenly know that they are completely alone…

Der Stern über dem Walde. 1904

Richard Schaukal

ANDREAS VON BALTHESSER TO COUNTESS F—

Dear Lady F—,

From your enviable rural seclusion, you ask me for a tale of adventure. I give you this, and one of the kind I like best: the ironic kind.

Yesterday evening, my manservant came in (I had dined at the Trautensteins at four, drunk my tea at six, and was about to dress for the Opera), and when I reluctantly turned to see what it was he wanted (I do not like surprises and Benedikt—unless summoned—respects my strict instructions to inflict his presence on me as seldom as possible), he announced, in the sober manner I have endeavoured, with inordinate patience, to inculcate, that Mr von Haller wished to speak to me immediately. I realised straight away that I was doomed to make an uncomfortable toilet, uncomfortable because it would be observed (which to my mind would necessarily make it imperfect); and that I would miss the beginning of *Carmen*—or the overture, at the very least—and would enter my box when the house lights had already been dimmed, a thing I absolutely detest because it prevents one from getting one's bearings. I also knew that Ernst Haller, a noisy sort of fellow, painfully awkward in his address, would unsettle me and perhaps destroy my entire mood, which I had laboured to keep sanguine during the course of a none too satisfactory day. I was extremely annoyed and, letting my hand fall from my dressing-room door handle, burst out (my discomposure distressed me, but the smoothly shaven chin of my manservant had reminded me all too powerfully of my own state of undress):

'And you said I was at home?'

'You gave no orders to say otherwise, Sir.'

'You ass, you must never admit that I am at home!'

I was immediately vexed at having spoken thus; the response had not been thought out, it had merely been provoked by that tyrannical desire to contradict which a master always feels towards his servant.

But Ernst von Haller was already standing in the doorway (he has a way of tearing doors open that makes one want to reach for one's riding crop). I collected myself with difficulty.

'Good evening,' I said, turning to face him.

I was struck at once by the disarray of his attire. Von Haller, after all, is one of the few people who know how to dress here (those people can be counted on the fingers of one hand) yet now, there he stood in my doorway with the untidy *chevelure* of an artist or a university student. His overcoat and frock coat hung unbuttoned and his hat had not been brushed (I could tell this by the way the lights above the looking-glass were reflected on its surface). Haller had entered unbidden and Benedikt remained hovering, visibly pale. But I did not want to dismiss him straight away. Reluctantly, I was anticipating an interview (how I hate that word! But interview it inevitably would be) and I wanted to tone the mood of its preamble down, from excitable volatility to the level of a social how-d'ye-do. But Ernst Haller did not give me the chance to make so much as an opening bid. Abruptly and almost theatrically, he announced:

'I must speak to you as a matter of urgency!'

At that point, I had the presence of mind to wave Benedikt away, otherwise the fellow would have taken delivery of a free instalment from the realm of the daily newspaper and the circulating library novel.

'You may go.'

When he had retreated, swiftly and silently (I never permit him to wear shoes that have been freshly re-heeled; how he arranges this is his own affair), I offered Haller my hand, a hand which I had not yet readied for the evening (once I have bathed and balmed my fingers, I never let anything come near them except in gloves), and indicated one of the two large leather armchairs beside the fireplace, with its subtle adornment of a wrought-iron screen. Haller threw himself onto its wide seat, between the high armrests, in such a way that the upholstery protested, but then immediately, as if he could not bear to sit still, bounced up again like an acrobat, almost into my face. I offered him my cigarette case—he had begun spluttering a lot of vague words—but he waved it away.

Planting himself in front of me like a man at a fencing lesson, he curtly and briefly—by now I was expecting it—asked about my relations with his sister.

'I know everything!' he cried (the silliest way of trying to bait me). And then, like a ball of string coming unravelled, the whole long-winded story came tumbling out.

It is well known that he has always mistrusted his sister. I even had a suspicion—well-founded, as I now saw—that he had had us watched. But I was irritated by the—as I have said, theatrical—manner in which he was staging this utterly pointless confrontation.

Baroness Alice Sigmar-Bouvelle is one of those women who—how shall I put it?—simply can't help it. She is very beautiful, tall and well-made, one of those insatiable blondes who so delectably know how to hide a voracious ardour (*très amusant*) behind a weary—shall we say, languor? When all is said and done, I care as little for her as I do for my watch-chain. But the grace with which she contemplates a smouldering cigarette through half-closed eyelids, her arm lightly draped across a cushion; or the way she springs lightly from the palm of the hand one has placed beneath her dainty foot, then swings herself round and slips into the saddle; these things please me beyond measure. So once, when she held out her hand to me, I took that hand and turned it over and planted a little kiss on it through the small hole where her glove fastens. And after that, it was plain sailing. It wasn't an affair that required much effort. But—loth as I always am to bring a comfortable arrangement to an end—I soon got bored with the whole thing. And now her brother had descended on me and was making all this preposterous fuss!

I lit a cigarette—it was now inevitable that I would be late for the Opera; and after all the talk that was certain to follow, I would need to give my teeth another thorough brushing. I lit my cigarette calmly (although I could feel myself starting to tremble slightly from the chest upwards) and—I know exactly what slow words to use—said merely: 'Are you saying you want a fight?' That always works famously.

Haller—thank God—paused for a moment in his incessant peregrinations between the fireplace and my desk, and turned to look at me (I noticed that his moustache needed trimming).

'I want certainty!' he said, very loudly.

Yet again, a word from the playwright's lexicon.

'What kind of "certainty"?' I asked, leaning back in my chair and letting the thin, blue-grey cigarette smoke filter out through my nose in short puffs.

'Certainty that you and my sister...'

He couldn't bring himself to say it. I didn't blame him. It would have been utterly fatal for me, too.

'My dear friend,' I said, sitting up a little straighter (my neck had been pressed uncomfortably tightly against my shirt collar), 'don't take it amiss, but you're—well, I'm sorry to say it, but you're being absurd.'

'Don't push me too far!' the poor fool blurted.

I had to smile. Haller, that lumbering old weather-vane, talking of being 'pushed'!

'In any case, you said you knew everything,' I reminded him.

And then (predictably!) he committed the gross imprudence of retorting, 'And so I do!'

I stood up. I thrust my hands into my trouser pockets.

'Dear chap, forgive me if I allow myself to—to whisper something rather naughty.' I raised my voice a little. 'You see, the thing is, I was rather hoping you would turn out to know "everything" so that I could be in on the secret too.'

He was clearly surprised. But I had got into my stride.

'After all,' I went on, 'the Baroness *does* have a husband.'

He said nothing. I offered him a cigarette. Rather distractedly, he took it.

'Look here, Ernst,' (I now took the risk of using his first name, at the same time wondering whether to ask Benedikt to bring us some brandy), 'Look here, Ernst, you're—I'm sorry to be blunt—you're being a damn fool. Don't embarrass yourself. If we told Fredi about this conversation,' (Fredi, Baron Alfred Sigmar-Bouvelle, is the happy guardian of my 'little flame'), 'he would split his sides laughing.' (I chose this 'chummy' expression because I was now sure of being able to salvage at least part of my beloved *Carmen* overture.) 'He would simply split his sides laughing.'

Ernst Haller sat down.

I had some brandy brought in. We smoked in silence. At last, he asked me to forgive him. I forgave him wholeheartedly. Then he came with me into my dressing-room. It was left to me to be gracious and to add the finishing touch. I invited him to accompany me to the Opera, upon which he sent for brushes and a comb and made himself look somewhat more human.

Wouldn't you say that was an adventure? Though I confess I should not want to exchange it for any of the famous stagecoach robberies in those romantic parts of the world that are still so popular because they are slowly ceasing to exist. You will no doubt be surprised that I have given the full names of the parties involved; even more so since they are names you will be hearing for the first time—you, dear Lady F—, who pride yourself on being so peculiarly well-informed when it comes to the people and the goings-on in society. Well, then, forgive me—forgive me for giving you no cause for alarm: I made them all up.

I remain, your ever respectful,

Andreas Balthesser

Andreas von Balthesser an die Gräfin F. 1907

Alexander Roda Roda

THE CONSEQUENCES OF A NON-REGULATION COLLAR

Rudi Meder totted up his money and saw that he had just enough. A Sunday afternoon certainly sets a man back!

Until 4 o'clock: Billiards at the Café Kaisergarten	20 *kreuzer*
4:30: meet Rosa on the Schillerplatz and walk in the Prater—pausing outside the Drittes Kaffeehaus (where you don't have to pay to listen to the music)	–
Two return trips to the city, at 10 *kreuzer* each	20 *kr.*
Dinner for two at the 'Grüner Baum' in the Schleifmühlgasse, twice 40 *kreuzer* – in total	80 *kr.*

10:30: fond farewells.	10 *kr.*
She goes back to Währing,	
he (gallant as ever) pays for	
her ticket	
Return trip to the Military Academy	10 *kr.*
Grand total	1 *fl.* 40 *kr.*

He would just have enough—but only just.

'Oi, you—cadet!' a nasal voice suddenly shouted. 'You there, cadet—hang about!'

Meder stood to attention at a respectful distance, saluted and choked back the knot of fear that had lodged itself in his throat.

His sergeant-major looked him up and down for a long time: half an hour for the cap; half an hour for the collar; a few minutes for the midriff and the legs; then slowly back to the collar. At last he said,

'That—that—harrumph! That collar of yours is at least six centimetres high. I mean to say, do you call that a collar?'

Meder said nothing.

'Eh? I mean—well, it looks more like a flipping bandage! Go home now and report yourself tomorrow for a non-regulation collar!'

The sergeant-major finished speaking, waggled a finger, and left.

Meder left too. Back to barracks.

Hm. The Café Kaisergarten would still be manageable. But Rosa? What would she do all on her own? Today—and on the five or six following Sundays when he would no doubt be confined to barracks with an old, tattered copy of the *Leipzig Illustrated Gazette*?

He told everyone in the mess room about his adventure, handed in his eleven o'clock card and then set to thinking about how to let Rosa know. Should he write? That wouldn't work. She lived in Währing[3], she was probably already on her way into town.

Silberer, one of the first-year recruits, went by.

'Oi, you—Silberer!' Rudi called out, imitating the sergeant-major as closely as he could.

Silberer had just received his eleven o'clock card and was scared stiff. But this time, Meder didn't pull rank; he simply asked casually, 'Are you up to anything in particular?'

No, Silberer was up to nothing in particular.

'Could you possibly be at the Schillerplatz at half past four? A lady is coming… Blonde, pretty, medium height. She'll be in a light blue dress with a Girardi boater[4]. She's called Rosa. Could you let her know that I can't make it?'

'But of course, delighted. Schillerplatz, half past four? You can count on me.'

'She's a lady, you understand? A lady. You mustn't—well, you know…'

'Pff! As if I don't know how to treat a lady!'

Silberer went to Leidinger's first, ate *filet à la Chateaubriand* and an omelette, drank a bottle of Saint-Estèphe, and finished off with a mocha and a Gianaclis cigarette[5].

Then the little restaurant clock struck four. He paid, ordered a rubber-wheeled cab and, while waiting for it to arrive, spent the time arranging his hair. The head waiter helped him into the cab.

'Schillerplatz!'

'What number does the Baron wish me to stop at?'

'No number. Just Schillerplatz,' said Silberer and leaned back against the seat. He was very curious to know what *she* would be like.

She, Rosie, was standing in front of the bust of Anastasius Grün[6], just looking at the time, when to her surprise, a completely unknown man from the Military Academy came up to her.

'Excuse me, are you Miss Rosa?'

Rosie blushed and simpered. 'Yes.'

'Mr Rudi Meder has had a visit from his uncle and sends his apologies for not being able to let you know earlier. He—he wonders if—well, if you could make do with me instead?' As he said this, Silberer pulled out his gold watch.

'Ooh!' said Rosie. 'Well, I'm sure I don't know. I rather wonder if I didn't ought to go back to Währing…'

Silberer waved a hand. A cab pulled up.

'Is this your conveyance?' Rosie asked.

Silberer invited her to take a seat with another wave of the hand. Rosie smiled blissfully and did so.

'Währing!'

The carriage rolled away from the kerb.

'Oh my, how quietly it goes! An 'orse-drawn carriage and

all! I ain't never been in an 'orse-drawn carriage before.'

She had never been to the Art Show[7] either, and it soon turned out that she was very partial to strawberries and cream and that she had no objection at all to having gone to the Art Show and to having eaten strawberries and cream there, instead of going home to Währing.

'What would you like to drink, Rosie?' asked Silberer as they sat listening to the Schrammel[8] band. 'Chocolate, perhaps?'

'Oh, I say, Hans!' She gurgled and clung to his arm so tightly that it made him feel a little clammy. She was simply in heaven: the horse-drawn carriage, the Schrammel band with its high-G clarinet, the strawberries and cream—and now she was to have chocolate. And dear, good, noble, handsome, nicely turned-out Hans as well, of course—oh, heavens, it was all so very different from what she was used to!

It was eight o'clock. She had seen so many things for the first time—tasted them, enjoyed them—and her head was spinning with happiness. And now they were on their way to the Stefanskeller[9].

Hans had been there a good few times with his cousin and he knew the ropes. The waiter silently opened the door of a *chambre séparée*—and in they slipped. And when the door closed behind them, the last barriers came down as well. In an ecstasy of happiness, Rosie threw her arms around her Hans's neck and kissed him and kissed him—and he kissed her back. Three hours later, in his army bunk, he found himself still dreaming about those kisses. Whereas she, at the same time in her bed in Währing, dreamt of ice cream and chocolate, Hans, strawberries, horse-drawn carriages, music and champagne…

It had been too wonderful. Much, much too wonderful.

The next Sunday, in the Café Kaisergarten, Rudi Meder strapped his cadet's sabre to his waist and sallied forth to the Schillerplatz.

He had got off lightly: the thing with his collar had only cost him a simple reprimand. Now, naturally, he wanted to meet up with Rosie and be twice as good a sport as usual; his allowance had been paid that morning.

Rosie arrived. A little late—but in a brand new silk blouse and with imitation-diamond studs winking in her ears. Hans had sent them to her the day before.

My, my, how elegant! marvelled Rudi. They exchanged greetings and set off on their usual walk. But as they passed the Imperial, where the horse-drawn cabs stood waiting for fares, Rosie suddenly decided that she couldn't take a step further because her shoes were too tight.

Rudi was astonished and stared at her feet.

'But your shoes have never been too tight before.'

'My feet are like blocks of ice.'

'In May? Well, all right, we can take the tram,' he said, instinctively trying to steer her away from the cabs.

But the damage had already been done.

'Where to, Sir?' called a coachman genially.

In no time at all, Rosie had hopped in and was leaning back against the seat, quite the woman of the world, inviting Rudi to join her.

He got in too. He hadn't even had time to think before Rosie gave the order:

'To the Drittes Kaffeehaus.'

'My word! Why not straight to the Sacher[10]?'

'Would you rather we went to the Sacher? Well, I'm sure I don't mind if I do,' Rosie replied coolly, in deliberate High German.

When they arrived, Rudi paid with a sigh and was almost rude when the coachman asked if he should wait for the young lady and gentleman. Silently, he did the arithmetic:

Melange and two *kipfel*[11] for Rosie	29 *kreuzer*
A glass of beer for himself	12 *kreuzer*
Grand total, with tip	1 *krone*.

And then supper on top? No. Today, Rosie would be sent home early.

But things turned out quite differently. Rosie immediately ordered iced coffee and then had waffles to go with it—waffle after waffle. And as she ate, she bobbed her head in time to the music, and laughed and chatted and made merry. She seemed ready to do anything in the world, in fact, other than be sent home early.

And of course, iced coffee and waffles don't amount to a square meal.

At first, Rudi tried not to hear her when she mentioned how hungry she was—but he couldn't keep it up forever. Tentatively he suggested getting a couple of sixpenny sausages from Salamutschi's. The look Rosie gave him was so scornful—so scornful that he lost the courage to make any further suggestions along those lines. Rosie had been looking forward to fried chicken all week, and fried chicken was what she absolutely must have. And if he didn't want to let her have it, well—well, that wouldn't be at all nice of him. Because if she had known that he begrudged her even the teeniest, tiny little whim—well… And so on and so forth.

Rudi sighed. 'Well, since the evening's already turned into a shambles…' He leaned back in his chair and ordered fried chicken with fruit compote, followed by *Doboschtorte* and a bottle of Goldeck[12].

Rosie sipped and munched and hummed along to the Schrammel music and in between called him a bore and a penny-pincher.

Yes, he *was* a penny-pincher. So much for his monthly allowance! It was ten o'clock and high time to go home. The worst of it all, though, was that he felt he had lost his power over Rosie. It had cost him the very last vestige of that former power to persuade her to go home to Währing by tram… Rosie had certainly learned to take a fellow to the cleaner's.

But where had she learned it from? From whom? Rudi thought about it all the way back to barracks.

Where from? From whom? She worked as a seamstress out in the suburbs. She never came into Vienna during the week. Her parents were both day labourers. It certainly wouldn't have been from them that she had learned about ice cream and *Doboschtorte*. And as for driving around in a horse-drawn cab! He had always told her that it was only counts and princes who drove around in cabs—and she had believed him. What had brought on this sudden change?

And then it occurred to him: Silberer. So *that* was why the wretch had been avoiding him recently. *That* was why…

Just you wait! Rudi thought. Revenge is sweet. Just you wait, Silberer!

During drill the next day, Rudi Meder ordered his nemesis to report 'for indolence'.

During the break that followed, though, he found himself walking up and down, deep in thought. Then, making up his mind, he went up to Silberer, grabbed him by the coat buttons, and said,

'You—you just pay more attention next time, d'you hear? And—well—you can forget about reporting yourself.'

And he was gone. Silberer watched him go in astonishment.

But then Sunday came, and Rudi had his chance. When Silberer was signing out, going off duty for the afternoon, Rudi said,

'You double-crossed me with Rosie. Not that I'm going to hold it against you. But you—you spoiled her. That's an underhand thing to have done.'

There was silence for a while. Then Hans asked,

'And—Rosie?'

'Oh,' said Rudi, 'she's expecting you at the Schillerplatz at half past four.'

Die Folgen eines zu hohen Kragens. 1908

Marie von Ebner-Eschenbach

THE POETRY OF THE UNWITTING

A short novella in a series of greetings cards

7th July

Dear Mother,

The château lies on top of a mountain. By our standards, it seems like a veritable Mont Blanc but here, alongside all these giants, it is just a little baby hillock. A green valley opens up to the east, with a stream running through it, as white as frothed-up soap suds. When I step out onto the balcony, a sea of green treetops swishes at my feet. 'Listen to them,' said Albrecht, 'they're welcoming you.' Wasn't that sweet? My husband is so good! I'm only now beginning to make his acquaintance. You have sent me off into the world with a perfect stranger.

I kiss your hands. There are a thousand tender things I'd like to say to you, but you don't like it when I do that, so I'll just say: Adieu!

Your loving Daughter

10th July

Dear Mother,

Thank you for your dear, sweet letter. It seems so unkind that in answer to it, I am using only one of the beautiful greetings cards you gave me. But I have so much to do. I want to become a lady of the manor, just like my mother; a support and a refuge for everything and everyone around me. Of course, you have been the mistress of your household for a very long time and I am just beginning to get used to being in charge. Albrecht frequently reproves me. 'Stop saying please all the time!' he says. 'A colonel tells his soldiers to "Forward march!" If he said, "Would you mind terribly if I asked you to march forward?" then half of them probably wouldn't budge.' But the situations aren't quite the same, are they, darling Mamma?

I embrace you. I'm sending my whole heart with—or should that be *in*?—this card.

13th July

Dear Child,
Stop worrying about the silly greetings cards and don't protest against my instructions. There are very good reasons why I do not wish to receive long letters from you in the first year of your marriage, reasons which your husband, the 'perfect stranger'—who is so well known to me—will certainly appreciate; you need only ask him.

Your sincerely affectionate Mother

17th July

Dear Mother,
I showed Albrecht your card and said: '*Do* you appreciate them, these reasons?' Oh, Mamma, he looked at me so gravely that I felt quite flustered. 'Of course,' he replied. Oh,

Mother, I fear my husband understands you better than I do! I did not dare ask him for an explanation. I still feel a little inhibited by him. He speaks so seldom, he is such a closed book: this getting to know him is not going nearly as quickly as I thought it would. There is something so vastly imposing about him, so tall and taciturn as he is. Am I not too small and insignificant for him, a foolish girl like me, who has seen so little of the world and understands so little of its ways?

22nd July

Dear Mother,
I decided I should try to amuse him. Oh, I have never seen him so bored! I hardly see him during the day; he spends all his time in the forest or at the estate office. He only comes in to dine at seven o'clock. And after dinner he smokes and reads the papers—and then the great silence commences. Once or twice I followed your advice and hazarded a few remarks, about books and suchlike. He listens to me patiently, but then he doesn't think it worth his while to respond to my chatter. And who can wonder at it? A man like him! A chit like me!

26th July

Dear Mother,
Three days ago, I made an attempt to draw him into conversation and asked him straight out: '*Wallenstein* or *Götz*, which do you prefer?' 'It's hard to say,' he said, pulling a grave face and looking for all the world like someone who is trying to steel himself for something. At last, he said: 'A book I like very much is *The Seven Years' War* by Schiller. Do you

know it?' 'No, I don't,' I told him, 'and neither does anyone else.' 'Why not?' 'Because it doesn't exist.' 'Really?' His brown cheeks got browner still; that is his way of blushing. Did it annoy him that I didn't fall in with his joke? Did I commit an even worse *gaucherie*? In any case, he stood up, made a remark about the weather, and then went out. And since then he has gone out every evening and I hardly see him any more. Oh, if only I hadn't said anything!

26th July

Dear Sister,

Things are not going as they should. My wife is perfection itself: in sweetness, in understanding, in erudition—in short, in every respect. She is much too good for me, and her opinion of me is also much too high!

The scales will fall from her eyes and then I shall have lost everything, for her love means everything to me; that love which she has bestowed on me in trusting good faith.

A man who chooses his wife ill is much to be pitied; I have chosen too well and am to be pitied most of all.

Albrecht

28th July

Dear Mother,

Yesterday, Albrecht and I went for a ride through the valley. It is very narrow for quite a long distance but then it suddenly opens out and one finds oneself amid meadows with a small lake, which is fed by our forest stream. On the shore of the lake is a garden, and in it a darling little château.

'Whose château is that?' I asked. 'Who lives there?' 'A Count Wiesenburg lived in it.' 'Lived?' 'Yes. He died recently. In Ems.' 'Was he a bachelor?' 'No.' 'And his widow?' 'She plans to take up residence abroad.' 'And this lovely house?' 'It is empty; it is to be sold.' 'It can't be empty! The flag is flying from the roof. The Countess must be in residence…' Then I saw how wary I should be of contradicting him, especially…

Forgive me, Mother, I'm going to ignore your instructions today and start a second card.

(28th July, continued)
…especially when he is wrong, as he was yesterday, because we met a little farmer fellow coming along the track, and he soon confirmed my suspicions: Countess Blanca von Wiesenburg has come home. 'You see?' I called out. Albrecht said nothing. He just began gnawing at his moustache and worrying at his horse. At last I couldn't bear to watch him any longer and cried out, 'Albrecht, stop it, the poor creature! If only the wretched Countess were a million miles away!'

Oh, the look he gave me! Oh, Mamma, does a woman ever learn not to be afraid of her husband?

29th July

Darling Mamma,
I hear that Cousin Hans is back and is still in F.'s wife's clutches. Won't you have him come and visit you and appeal to his conscience? You are so good at that sort of thing. You can also tell him that we, Albrecht and I, are ashamed of him. Albrecht simply cannot understand how a man can be so dishonourable

as to run after another man's wife. You should have heard how upset he was when I asked him if he knew about the situation. 'What would *you* say to a man who had behaved thus?' he asked. Well, of course I hastened to reassure him. 'I should despise him!' I declared. 'He's dishonest and a liar and above all things a cheat!' 'And so he is indeed!' cried Albrecht, with an expression I can hardly describe. O Lord, how noble must a man be who feels so personally injured by the baseness of others! I got up and went to him and planted a kiss upon his honest brow. But he can't bear outbursts of tenderness any more than you can, and deep down I admire that quality in him. 'That's enough, let us forget it,' he said, and turned away.

29th July

Dear Sister,

I cannot get away, otherwise I should have brought my wife to meet you before now. I so much long for you to know her, but I am at present obliged to direct the affairs of my estate, and thus it will remain for some time to come. It is terrible how things have been mismanaged over the last few cursed years. But that is nothing; I can deal with it quite easily on my own. There is something else.

Blanca is here at the château!!!

So she has kept her word, and if my wife finds out, then everything is over for me—everything! And that is something I cannot deal with easily or on my own.

Dear sister, put your horses between the traces, jump into your carriage and come!

Albrecht

1st August

Dear Mother,

Albrecht's sister has paid us a surprise visit. She is ten years older than him, unmarried, and likely to remain so. She is tall and thin, very kind and extremely clever. She must have been a great beauty in her youth. Her eyes still are beautiful, and they seem to see straight through one. She makes very little of herself, her posture usually has something neglectful about it; but then sometimes, suddenly, she seems to recollect herself, and then she stands up straight. At such moments, next to her, I feel like a mere gnat. My Albrecht enjoys her company. Well—a man like him can easily hold his own among superior beings.

3rd August

Dear Mother,

My husband has become more talkative than usual, and Emilie, his sister, always knows what he means, even if he says the complete opposite (he seems exceedingly distracted at the moment). For example, he will suddenly mention the Orinoco or start talking about Charlemagne, but in the most muddled-up contexts. This does not discomfit Emilie in the slightest (in the way I was discomfited over that *Seven Years' War* business). She just nods in agreement and says, 'That's right, the Mississippi,' or, 'Yes, indeed, Charles V.' And he says, 'Exactly,' delighted that he has managed to make himself so clear.

So I will have to learn to deal with him like she does!

4th August

Dear Mother,

My sister-in-law went to call on Countess Wiesenburg on the very day of her arrival. She wanted to make up for a small omission on Albrecht's part, namely that he had forgotten to inform the Countess of his marriage, which seems to have upset her. Emilie was with her for some time, and my husband awaited her return with extraordinary anxiousness. I quite wished that I could suddenly find myself in danger, so that he would be similarly anxious about me.

When Emilie finally came back, I noticed that he was much less happy at her return than he had been anxious at her absence. He just said, 'All sorted out?' 'By no means. You must go and see her in person.' Albrecht protested, and I was glad to hear him do so. However extraordinary a woman his sister might be, it does not give her the right to tell my husband what he *must* do!

6th August

Dear Mother,

Countess Blanca has been to visit us. Picture to yourself a story-book Snow White with melancholy blue eyes and rippling, silken, ash-blonde hair. As my old music master would say (please give him my warmest regards): a harmonious composition. I was delighted with her at first sight, and she—oh Lord, never in the whole course of my life has anyone greeted me with such warmth! She is as excellent a person as Emilie, and her life has also been full of trials; she was unhappily married, she readily admits it. She is as trusting as a child, although she cannot be under thirty years of age. How sad that I am so soon to lose the friend I have barely begun to make! The little château has been sold and Blanca has only come here to strike camp.

8th August

Dear Mother,
Things have been rather peculiar here since Blanca arrived. She often comes to see me, wanting to talk to me alone. Well, if only Albrecht and Emilie would leave us to ourselves for half a minute! But I am constantly guarded and sheltered. I could not be better protected if Blanca were my mortal enemy, plotting my ruin. I am not naturally suspicious, but at the moment it seems that everything is conspiring to make me so.

10th August

Dear Mother,
Blanca must at some time have suffered a great disappointment because she is always alluding to it. 'There is no fidelity in the world!' she said today, and Emilie retorted: 'Everyone is free to prove the opposite. Practise fidelity and you will find it in the world.' Her eyes had a funny glint in them as she said this. But Blanca managed to hold her gaze (I can never do so without blinking furiously) and just smiled and said: 'I'll make use of the lesson. I am the kind of person who always sees her plans through. You don't imagine I have come here merely to pack up my effects, do you? I have come to see that justice is done—and done it shall be.' Emilie returned the smile but it seemed a little vinegary. 'Is it justice that you wish to see? Or

a denunciation?' 'Call it what you will,' said Blanca. 'In such cases,' Emilie replied, 'the denouncer often turns out to be an equally guilty party.' 'Ah, who knows? Perhaps everything, even the eagerness of the innocent and pure, merely sharpens such a person's thirst for revenge…'

Their exchange seemed rather childish to me, but they both seemed to speak so pointedly, as if a whole host of meanings were lurking behind every word.

12th August

Dear Mother,

Have I already mentioned that Blanca takes pleasure in teasing my husband? Well, it's true. I'm only surprised she has the nerve to do so. She teases him about—well, about this mental muddle that seems to have been afflicting him recently. She also claims that he has invented a new system of spelling. While putting various papers in order (presumably papers belonging to her husband), she came across some peculiar documents that she says she wants to show me—because of the spelling, she said. But she said it so strangely, her manner was so defiant, and Albrecht seemed so tremendously embarrassed by it, that I found myself quite vexed and exclaimed: 'Very well, bring them forth! I want to see them! I have no idea of my husband's writing style, as it happens. We have not had occasion to correspond during the course of our short married life. So out with these papers, if you please!' But then my husband reacted so vehemently. And this vehemence, together with his dark, louring expression… Oh! I love him more than I can say, but if this goes on, I will come to fear him even more than I love him—and that, Mamma, would be a terrible misfortune.

15th August

My honoured Mother-in-law,

I confirm with sincere thanks that I have safely received my dear wife's correspondence cards and recognise from this your good intentions. The situation is very hard. I have no idea how to prevent her from taking fright when my own fear on her account begins to show itself. The storm is gathering over my house; the lightning is about to strike. You know everything. I faithfully admitted everything to you before paying my addresses to your daughter—that is to say, to my dear wife and to her family. My nerves are completely in tatters. Should I relieve this tension by confessing everything to her?

She will despise me. Oh, please advise me! It will all come out. Words are the only means at my disposal for not making a dupe of my dear wife. It is enough that too much damage has already been done by concealment.

Advise me!

18th August

My dear Son-in-law,

I presume that you were not in earnest when you asked whether you should confess everything. Allow me, therefore, to dispense with the courtesy of a reply. And as for making a dupe of your wife, may I suggest, if you feel an aversion to the idea, that you endeavour to overcome it? For how can you govern if you cannot deceive? Is not the act of taking a wife synonymous with governorship? Has it not always been thus, since the world first began?

20th August

Honoured Mother-in-law,
Forgive me if I tell you that you are mistaken. I was in deadly earnest when I spoke of confessing. It is not as singular as it seems, for I know that 'a certain person' will not rest until that 'certain person' has betrayed me. But since this is your counsel, I will remain silent. May I never regret it—ah, but I shall live to do so!

Regret is a terrible thing.

I have become a coward in her clutches. There are other strings I could pull, it is true; but my sister keeps me from doing so. Otherwise I should already have taken decisive action.

22nd August

Dear Son-in-law,
Your sister is right; on no account should you take decisive action. You speak of 'a certain person' betraying you. In Heaven's name, what nonsense is this! If she betrays you, she betrays herself—and what more have you to do then than admit that you had the misfortune to be charmed by a coquette, immediately adding that in matters of the heart, a man may justifiably demand an account of his wife's past history but under no circumstances is he obliged to give any account of his own. Do not, if I may advise you, allow yourself

to be induced to offer justification, but content yourself simply with the 'It was ever thus' formula—for, paltry as this formula undoubtedly is, it nevertheless holds up well enough in a case that admits of few strong arguments. We all know full well that most coins possess nothing like the worth that they pretend—and yet their face value is universally accepted. I am sure that I make myself clear.

22nd August

Dear Mother,

Everything is going very well. We went to the little château—Emilie and I, that is—to say goodbye. Albrecht had promised to join us, but he did not come. He must be terribly busy again, I told myself, and made his excuses to Blanca. But after that, we had scarcely turned for home, when whom did I espy? None other than my husband, standing by the roadside, looking out for us (if I were completely truthful, I should say looking out for *me*), earnestly waiting like a male version of Penelope at her loom. When we drew alongside him, he jumped into the carriage, looked first at Emilie, who nodded at him as if in reassurance, and then at me and joyfully burst out, 'So you're here! Safely on your way home!' as if I were returning unharmed from battle or from a journey to a land infested with cannibals. 'What on earth were you afraid of?' I asked. 'The road is good and the horses are docile.'

Then he took my hands in his and panted out: 'Oh, my heart—to love is to fear!'

23rd August

Dear Mother,

She has gone, gone for good, alas. She appeared and then vanished again like a lovely apparition. At the last minute, Albrecht's conscience got the better of him and he drove to the station to bid her farewell in her railway carriage. He had a long way to go and there was no way he would be back before evening. Emilie stayed with me.

Oh, dear Mamma, they think I haven't got eyes in my head! They talk such stuff, while all the while I am royally enjoying their subterfuges! Albrecht didn't go to the station because he wanted to say goodbye to Blanca. He went because he wanted to make sure that she was really leaving. And Emilie does not pace up and down the terrace for her own pleasure, but because she is patrolling it like a sentry. And while all these careful precautions are being taken, the very thing they were trying to prevent happening has happened. Albrecht's letters to the Countess are in my hands. I have them! I have them!

Emilie is calling me, I must go to her. Adieu for now. I will send another card by the afternoon post.

23rd August, afternoon

Dear Mother,

I must tell you how I came by the letters. A little boy brought me a basket filled with beautiful roses. 'Who sent these?' Emilie wanted to know. 'The pastor?' 'Yes, that's right!' Nothing could be more natural. Only the other day we had stopped by the priest's garden and admired his display of Provence roses, and the basket was filled with them, tossed in just anyhow. I was enchanted. I took the flowers to my room to put them in water, and what did I find, hidden underneath them, but a note and a sealed package. I copy the note here:

'Delivering these letters to you will cost me dearly: I lose thereby your good opinion. Well: I pay the price; you shall reap the benefits. Life in general, and marriage in particular, is a struggle. I offer you some weapons. Blanca'

At the very moment when she is quitting us for good, she still finds the frame of mind for this mischievous joke. It shows sprightliness of character, I admit, and while what she writes is very spirited, I should have preferred a simple, warm farewell.

24th August

Darling Mother,
Today I must write you a proper long letter, and today you must forgive me and make allowances for it.

I'll tell you everything, right from the beginning, although it is only the ending that is really of interest.

Albrecht did not return until after nine o'clock last night. He stopped the carriage outside the gate and had already hurried into the house while I was standing at the window, afraid because a heavy thunderstorm was brewing. Then the door opened and Albrecht burst in. He startled me and I let out a little cry—and then he did the same.

'What is it? What's wrong? What has happened?' He looked about the room, took in everything at a glance, even the roses standing on the table next to the lamp, and I, because I always get nervous when he is overwrought like this, just blurted out, 'Blanca sent the roses. Your letters were with them.'

He flinched like a stricken deer, though he didn't say a word, he just began pummelling his head with both clenched fists.

'Albrecht! Albrecht!' I cried. 'How wrong of you, how terribly wrong!'

'Ah, how right you are!'

All he could do was groan and I don't know how it was that I stopped myself from bursting into tears at his pain, but I managed to say, admittedly in a very shaky voice, 'How wrong of you to want to keep secrets from me! How wrong that you don't want to reveal yourself to me as you are, with your good and upright character and your atrocious spelling!'

'You are making fun of me,' he managed to say at last, and I replied, 'Making fun of you? Why? Because you didn't have time to mug away at your books? A man like you, who has better things to do? Oh, my dear, why try to deceive me? What do I care whether you believe that the source of the Inster is in the Rhineland or that Catherine de' Medici was the wife of Peter the Great? If you could only know, and hold on to that knowledge for certain and never forget it, that I am and wish to be your dearest friend and confidante…' '

And *wish* to be?' he cut in, agape. '*Wish* to be?'

'Must I still wish it?' I cried. 'Am I not your wife?'

At which he asked, 'You say this now? Now—after reading…' He pointed to the packet of letters and trembled. He trembled all over—and indeed it was his good fortune that he did so, or else I should have flown into a towering and pitiless rage. But because he looked so ashamed and repentant, I only said, a little reproachfully, '*After* reading? Albrecht, how can you think so?'

'You mean you have not…? You did not…?'

'See for yourself whether the seal is unbroken,' I replied, my voice by now quite calm. And as I spoke, I put the packet of letters into his breast pocket. 'And in future,' I went on, 'never again believe it possible that I would knowingly do anything that distresses you.'

Well—now comes the interesting part! And I'll remember it as long as I live. Instead of being annoyed by my stern words, as I might have expected, instead of that… Oh, Mother, never before had he knelt before me, not as a suitor, not even on the first night of our honeymoon. But at that moment, before I knew what was happening, before I could do anything to stop it, he had prostrated himself at my feet. My dearest husband, my beloved master—and his hands were clasped as if he were at prayer. Fat tears glistened in his eyes, and he shouted out and whispered by turns, in boisterous jubilation and in quiet rapture: 'Oh, my wife! My darling child!'

Die Poesie des Unbewußten. 1914

Therese Rie

A PETTY BOURGEOISE

Elisabeth set off, as she did every afternoon, to pick her daughter up from school; and as she went on her customary way, her mind pursued its customary train of thought: that the price of meat would go up again, just as the butcher had said it would; that servants were getting more and more impudent; that if she could give it a new lining, her dark blue costume might do for a while longer, though it could certainly no longer be called fashionable. At which her thoughts wandered to Lady Rowena Springfield, who, in the latest instalment of the serialised novel in the *Abendblatt* (translated from the English), had drawn herself up to her full height and declared to her husband, 'Wretch! My revenge on you is now complete!' But since the instalment had ended there, readers had to wait until the following day to find out exactly what it was that Lady Rowena had done to him. From this, Elisabeth's thoughts turned to her own husband, and she was forced to admit that the Professor had seemed tetchier and more absent-minded than ever lately, and that it was a long time since he had paid her the remotest attention. And then, just as Elisabeth's thoughts were about to come full circle and go back to the butcher again, she realised that a man was staring at her.

It was a long and admiring stare. Almost unconsciously, it filled Elisabeth with satisfaction, since it came at the very moment when she had been beginning to think that her husband's indifference was something to worry about. She was reminded of her physical attractions. Though too unrefined to be precisely beautiful, she was tall and curvaceous, with golden hair and a fresh complexion. As a girl, she had once been cast as Germania in a *tableau vivant*, and it was on that occasion that the Professor had fallen in love with her. That was eight years ago now but at the time he had been truly in love with her, as she had been with him, and in her simple mind, Elisabeth had imagined that such a state of affairs between husband and wife could never change.

She went into a haberdasher's and bought a reel of thread, and as she came out she saw that the stranger had followed her and that he was still following her. This disconcerted her and she felt that it was making her look awkward. It was not the first time that she had had an 'admirer' of this kind but the persistence of this one surprised her. She walked on very quickly and got to the school too early, so that she had to wait a few minutes. The man stationed himself on the other side of the road and continued to stare, surreptitiously but fixedly. And now, whether she wanted to or not, Elisabeth had to look at him, too. He was good-looking. Of medium height, slim, with pale grey eyes that contrasted oddly with the deep black of his lashes and brows. His somewhat loud purple cravat went well with his olive skin and dark moustache. His bearing was elegant and he even had a pair of brand new light yellow gloves, which made Elizabeth uncomfortably aware that her own string ones had been darned several times at the fingertips.

The school bell rang and the children came out in twos. Little Mizl threw herself into her mother's arms. At that point her pursuer disappeared too, but Elisabeth was still so taken up with her adventure that as soon as she got home, she called out to her husband, 'Just think, someone followed me in the street today!' The Professor winced, as he always did when he was engrossed in his work and someone disturbed him. But Elisabeth had something else interesting to tell him, too. 'The price of meat is going up again, if you can believe it.' And when he still didn't respond, she played her trump card: 'Mali broke another coffee cup today. That makes three in a week. I gave her her notice. What a cross one has to bear with servants these days!' The Professor still did not react. He just stared mournfully at his manuscript, as if in pain, as if he couldn't wait for her to stop talking. It is too bad—a husband who takes no interest in anything! thought Elisabeth, vexed, and took herself off to the kitchen.

She pictured her husband's fine profile, hunched over his books, and sighed. She still liked her husband better than any other man, but it was a shame his income was so meagre. He was an associate professor at the University, a non-stipendiary position. What money he had came from a small college teaching salary plus the earnings of an academic paper here and there and a few private lectures. It meant that they lived extremely modestly. When Elisabeth thought of her sister, who had married a rich textile merchant from Linz! Of course, she liked her Professor a thousand times better than the fat textile merchant. Except that her Professor no longer looked at her. But why didn't he? She was an attractive young woman, and a good housekeeper, not a spendthrift. What would a dreamy, head-in-the-clouds man like him do without someone like her? He had always known she wasn't interested in all his ancient Egyptian stuff; she had made that perfectly clear as soon as they got engaged and he had just laughed. Honestly! She took the tray through to the front room and said in her loud, cheerful voice, 'Coffee's ready! A nice fresh cup of coffee!'

The Professor pulled his pained face again. 'My dear, can't you see that I'm working very hard? Why must you always disturb me?'

His tone was mild but she could tell that it was a forced mildness. It was the kind of tone one takes with an unruly child, a child who can't help its own bad behaviour, and this annoyed Elisabeth much more than a violent outburst would have done.

'Then you can jolly well drink your coffee cold!' she said, going angrily back into the kitchen. She sat down at the table and crumbled a roll into her cup. Drinking coffee was an important business. When a person loses their taste for coffee, that's the end. That's what her late mother used to say.

The Professor's apartment consisted only of a dining-room and bedroom, adjoined by a small room where Mizl slept. The dining-room also served as the Professor's study and, according to an agreement, it was only to be used by the others at mealtimes, because at all other hours, the Professor needed to work completely undisturbed. But today, Elisabeth took a perverse pleasure in continually going in and out, rattling around in the sideboard and clattering the bone china, because she could see how much it was annoying her husband. He didn't say anything, but after a while he got up.

'I'm going to the Science Society tonight,' he said.

And off he went.

Elisabeth stood there, stunned. And if the concierge's wife hadn't at that moment come up to complain that a duster had been dropped from the Professor's window again this morning, there was no knowing what would have happened. Instead, Elisabeth turned her anger on the concierge's wife, because even though what the woman said was perfectly true, Elisabeth couldn't afford to concede it. Otherwise, one never sees the back of such people…

The next morning, when Elisabeth took Mizl to school, something strange happened. 'He' was there again, standing outside her front door as if he had nothing better to do but loiter around waiting for her. As long as she was with her daughter, he kept a respectful distance. But no sooner had she dropped her off at school than she heard his footsteps close behind her. She hurried on to the nearby market. Elisabeth made a point of doing her own shopping; the servants just took any errand as an opportunity to diddle her. But the presence of her pursuer flustered her and the market women were understandably astonished that the Professor's wife, who normally drove such a hard bargain, accepted their prices almost without demur. As she turned to go home with her bulging bag, she heard the man's voice at her elbow:

'Madam!' And then, more pleadingly: 'Just one word, dearest Madam!'

But Elisabeth did not look at him. Usually, the best way to shake off a pursuer is to ignore him, she knew that, and a respectable housewife such as herself had to ignore such a man. She felt as if she could still hear his footsteps on the stairs as she ran up the four flights. Breathing hard, with beads of sweat upon her brow, she shut the door fast.

What she dearly wanted was to tell the Professor about her adventure straight away, but he seemed so unapproachable that she decided not to. She had barely changed her blouse and tied on her apron when the doorbell rang. 'Don't open it!' she wanted to call to Mali, but it was too late. Mali came back. 'A messenger has brought a letter for you, Ma'am,' she said. Elisabeth tore open a large, pale green, heavily perfumed envelope and read as follows:

Madam! I know that my presumption is reprehensible, but I am possessed by an urge so overpowering that I know you will forgive. I request and desire nothing more from you but this: permit me to speak to you just once. If what I say offends you, I will disappear from your life forever. I will wait for you, and will know from your face whether I may speak to you. Oh, do not refuse me! Yours, A.B.

When Elisabeth had read the letter, she felt so restless and confused that she decided to send Mali to fetch her daughter from school at midday. In any case, she could not have gone herself because her sister—a different sister—was coming to visit. This sister, who was married to a tax inspector, was very proud of her learned brother-in-law and sought every opportunity to be in his company. Today was no exception and she took a seat in the dining-room, in spite—or rather because of—the fact that she knew the Professor was working there. She constantly tried to bring him into the conversation but the Professor, who was far too meek to be anything but patient and polite, just let the stream of chatter flow over his head. Only once did he seem to pay any attention, and that was when the two women mentioned a cousin's impending divorce.

They condemned this course of action out of hand: what had come together should stay together, they opined. But the Professor said, 'If two people realise that they are incompatible, they should go their separate ways.' He said it so decisively, in a tone so unlike his usual vague way of speaking, that Elisabeth was momentarily taken aback. She remembered that they had talked about this subject a few weeks ago and that the Professor had said something similar. Only she hadn't remarked on it then—it was typical of her, in fact, not to notice things until after the event. But now she asked herself: is my husband planning to divorce me? Her eyes slid over his fine-featured, pale, indecisive face and at once she felt reassured. No, he was not the man for such a thing. Quite apart from the fact that she had never given him the slightest cause to wish for it. He had too much of a horror of fuss to be able to contemplate something like that.

After lunch, the Professor usually took their daughter back to school on his way to the Imperial Court Library. Elisabeth took the opportunity to have a nap: she had been up since dawn and was tired after the morning's chores. The apartment was very quiet at this hour, with just the soft clinking sound of Mali washing up in the kitchen. But Elisabeth couldn't sleep today. There was something in the air that kept her awake, she didn't know quite what. She went out a little earlier than usual, in need of sunshine and fresh air. When she got downstairs, 'He' was standing there.

He went towards her and tipped his hat politely. 'Madam, I am conscious of my audacity. But I beg you to hear me out. You need not say a word. Just listen to what I have to say.'

'What is it that you want?' Elisabeth asked curtly, half persuaded against her will.

'It is difficult to explain, Madam, what drew me to you. At first, perhaps, it was your fresh-faced loveliness. But there is something else. I beg you to believe that it is no ordinary cheap adventure that I seek, not one of those entanglements that you surely and rightly despise. But the more I see of you, the more I must adore you. Your cheerful diligence, your conscientiousness, your domestic virtue…'

He went on in this strain and Elisabeth listened. At last! she thought, not without satisfaction. Someone who appreciates me for who I am! He had fallen into step beside her and she noticed, again with satisfaction, that she was taller than him (she was taller than the Professor, too, as it happened; he had developed such a stoop). He told her all about his loneliness, about how he had grown up without parents or siblings and how he had always longed for truly feminine company. He also told her his name: Anton Brückler. When they neared the school, he kissed her hand fervently.

'You are a noble woman! You have done a good deed!'

'Oh, please!' stammered Elisabeth. The absence of any of the impertinence she had expected made it impossible for her to take the defensive stance she had planned.

'Will you permit me to ask one thing,? he said. 'May I come back tomorrow?'

Elisabeth made as if to refuse but he held up a hand. 'Just as we were today—no more than a quarter of an hour in the company of a beautiful, fine, intelligent woman.'

Elisabeth said nothing but she felt that her silence was not a refusal.

'How strange,' she thought, 'yesterday morning I had no idea that such a person as Anton Brückler existed and today—today I'm having something like an adventure!' And she felt that she was actually looking forward to it.

The next day he was there again, and so it went on, twice a day, every time she went out alone, which only ever happened on the way to or from Mizl's school.

'Don't you have a job? How is it that you have so much time?' she asked.

He smiled. 'Oh, I'm a civil servant. The Ministry doesn't make a fuss about my working hours.'

At first he only spoke to her, in the trusting, reverent tone which had captivated her from the first. He never risked a nearer approach; only once did he bring her a few roses. And by and by, she began to trust him, too. She had no girlfriends, no one who understood her. Mr Brückler seemed to appreciate the little cares of domestic life. He took such an interest and was so admiring of her prudence, her thriftiness. Incidentally, he turned out to know the Professor; he had once met him at the home of a Madame Stefani, the widow of an artist.

Elisabeth had only known her new friend for a few days but already it seemed to her a long time. Her days had become strangely rich. She found herself looking forward to their walks, which began to take them a lot further than just to the school and back—but they always went along different streets, so as not to give rise to any gossip. Elisabeth was insistent on that point. Once, however, she complained bitterly about her husband and Mr Brückler took her side.

'That dozy bookworm has no idea what a treasure he has in you!' he cried. 'You spend your whole life making him comfortable and he doesn't even notice!'

'That's true,' said Elisabeth with a sigh. 'I often think he's thinking about someone else.'

'Perhaps he is,' smiled Mr Brückler.

'What?' cried Elisabeth. 'Do you know something?'

'I don't know anything,' said Mr Brückler pointedly. 'I only know that Edith Stefani is mad about him. Some people think she is genuinely in love with him.'

'In love with my husband?' said Elisabeth indignantly.

It was not the first time she had heard the name Stefani. Madame Stefani was an aesthete, passionate about antiquities; scholars and artists were forever going to gatherings in her salon. The Professor went there from time to time, too, but Elisabeth had never been. She found it all far too dull. All her husband's acquaintance bored her; she kept them all at arm's length. She wished they knew a few smart, jolly couples with whom they could go out for a glass of beer or to a coffee house in the evening, or on an outing to Rodaun or the Wachau on Sundays. But the Professor had no desire to do anything of the kind, so they lived a very retired life.

'Is Madame Stefani beautiful?' Elisabeth asked.

'No, but interesting. And completely hard. Hard as nails and unscrupulous. What she wants, she gets,' said Mr Brückler.

'Do you think she wants my husband?' asked Elisabeth.

'I couldn't say,' said Mr Brückler gravely.

Elisabeth just laughed a boisterous laugh. 'I'd like to see her try.'

'Has your husband ever spoken to you about divorce?' Mr Brückler went on.

'Yes—no—I don't know,' said Elisabeth, unsure of herself. She remembered his remarks on the subject and didn't know what to think.

'A clever woman would actually beat the man to it,' Mr Brückler said, strangely serious.

Elisabeth looked at him. 'It doesn't appeal to me,' she said proudly. And she thought to herself: Of course, it might suit *you* if I got divorced!

Mr Brückler shrugged and changed the subject. He admired Elisabeth's new blouse, which she had made herself. She liked to listen to his compliments. She gave him a blow-by-blow account of how she had bought the fabric, very cheaply in a sale, and how the lace had come from a very old dress, and how she had made it look as good as new by washing it in benzene. Then they stopped in front of an outfitter's and inspected the goods on display. If only she could enjoy such simple pleasures with the Professor!

Gradually, Elisabeth's ideas began to change. She began to regard the few women she consorted with, including her two sisters, as philistines. These women's husbands—just like her own—had become indifferent to them over time. But none of these women had succeeded in acquiring such a fervent admirer of their charms as Elisabeth now had. She realised that Mr Brückler was slowly beginning to mean more to her, and silently she allowed it to happen. In deserted parks he sometimes brought her hand to his lips. And then came the first kiss…

She did not know whether she loved him. The Professor still seemed cleverer, more refined, more likeable. But her young, warm blood had been stirred and her Professor husband didn't seem to like *her*; indeed, she often felt that she was downright distasteful to him, whereas this other man desired her. She had known him for such a short time and yet he was already so firmly implanted in her life! Not that she knew anything about him. Neither where he lived nor how. He had told her one or two inconsequential things, but never anything real, anything concrete. She addressed him in the informal and called him Toni but she still didn't know where he lived or who his friends were.

The first time he asked her to visit him in his lodgings, she angrily pushed him away.

'What do you think I am?'

She went home earlier than usual. The *Abendblatt* lay on

the doorstep. She picked it up and suddenly remembered how long it had been since she had read about Lady Rowena Springfield. She flicked through the pages but they were serialising a different novel now so she would never know what became of Lady Rowena. But what did it matter, since her own life was now filled with wonderful things—things worthy of a novel in themselves?

The thought of Edith Stefani still tormented her, though.

'I should like to have the chance to see her,' she said, when Toni mentioned her name again.

'Nothing could be easier. She goes to all your husband's lectures. You must already have seen her.'

Elisabeth looked at him in astonishment. 'Me? I never go to those lectures. They're far too dull.'

'Well, he's giving one today. Shall we go?'

As a bride-to-be, she had once been to listen to her fiancé, when he was still a college tutor, but she had been so horribly bored that in the early days of their marriage she had happily taken refuge in the washtub whenever he asked her if she wanted to come to hear him speak. And then, of course, he had stopped suggesting it. The Professor would have been astonished to see his wife in the lecture hall today, but with his short sight he couldn't see further than the third row, and Elisabeth and Toni were sitting near the back.

'Where is Madame Stefani?' Elisabeth whispered.

Mr Brückler pointed to a woman at the very front. She turned around and Elisabeth could see her clearly. A slim, pale, brown-haired woman, no longer young, but very intelligent-looking and very sharp. I'm prettier, Elisabeth thought.

Then the Professor came in and the students stood up. Elisabeth noticed how his eyes met those of Madame Stefani. She paid no attention to her husband's lecture, nor would she have understood it. But the understanding between him and that woman annoyed her very much. For a moment, she wondered if she shouldn't rush over to him after the lecture and make a scene. But she knew him too well: it would mean the end of her marriage to do that.

A wild rage seized Elisabeth. So *that's* his companion, she thought. His soulmate! Here am I, working my fingers to the bone while he goes to see her to relax and exchange little ideas! All at once, she felt herself a martyr to unremitting housework, a sacrificial victim of her husband's need for domestic comfort. She looked at him. Could that man really excite an unknown woman to the heights of passion? That bloodless, undemonstrative, bookish man? And yet there was a time—she remembered it quite clearly—when she too had loved him fiercely. There must have been something in his smile, in the sound of his tentative voice, something that brought out her protective instinct, her instinct to cherish…

Then the unknown woman turned to face them. Her eyes seemed to signal to Toni, who discreetly bowed his head, then fixed his attention firmly on Elisabeth. Elisabeth could not bear the other woman's gaze. She felt a sense of something sinister, something that sent a chill down her spine. Then Madame Stefani turned away as if in contempt, as if she had realised that Elisabeth made a very paltry adversary. There could be no doubt that she knew who she was. Elisabeth felt a mute fury welling up inside her. She was not one to be deceived, to be betrayed behind her back, made fun of. Fortunately, she had the means to take revenge

'Let's go back to your lodgings,' she said, as she and Toni were making their way down the wide marble staircase.

'What did you say?' he asked, surprised.

'Let's go back to your lodgings. Didn't you invite me there yesterday? Well, today I want to go—so take me there.'

'I can't today,' he said, embarrassed. 'I'm terribly sorry. I'm a bachelor, you see, and everything's in a terrible mess. But tomorrow—tomorrow with pleasure!' And he kissed her hand fiercely.

But when Elisabeth returned home, to the bourgeois atmosphere that was the backdrop of her existence, she regretted having been so rash. She would have liked to forget all about it. And if the Professor had been warm and receptive to her that evening, as he had been in the first years of their marriage, nothing would have happened. But he wasn't and Elisabeth felt her defiance growing.

The next day, she pondered the question of what to wear. Although no French novels had ever crossed her consciousness, her feminine instinct nevertheless spoke to her of a *toilette de circonstance*, about lace and delicate-coloured ribbons. But the only clothes she had were of coarse, joyless, sober linen. Yet her frugal mind forbade her to buy anything new for this occasion—this one and only occasion, she told herself. It was already too late, so she decided that her beautiful hair and her strong, healthy body were adornment enough. Deep down, she had little desire to go, but anger, jealousy, curiosity and her awakened sensibilities drew her on.

But as if fate were conspiring to prevent it, a number of things happened to make her progress difficult. The Professor suddenly spoke to her sweetly and kindly. Mizl clung to her neck and didn't want to let her go. It began to rain. And when she finally got to the tram, there was a traffic incident that caused a long delay.

When at last she arrived, flustered and heated, at Toni's lodgings—a mezzanine room in Wieden[13]—Toni greeted her with something less than enthusiasm. 'So late!' he grumbled, looking at his watch.

'Why? Do you have plans after all?' asked Elisabeth, offended. She had expected an ardent reception.

'Oh, but you must understand! When one has waited so long and so eagerly, one's nerves are worn to rags!'

But his voice sounded far from eager; in fact, it seemed sober and business-like. Elisabeth wanted to enjoy her adventure, wanted to drink in every feature of his rather dreary room with its oil prints, its surfeit of rugs, the paper fans and the somewhat cloying smell, but Toni was very impatient. He was in such a hurry, in fact, that he didn't offer her any of the sweetmeats that were set out on a side table and which Elisabeth would dearly have liked to taste. She did not feel in the least aroused. In common with most middle-class women, the fact that she had come to him, that she had now seen his *milieu*, meant that for her, the main thrill was over. But he urged her on with almost brutal haste. I don't really love him at all, she thought, as he kissed her, in the most workmanlike way. The fact is, I much prefer my husband…

Then, something appalling happened. She heard her husband's voice. She thought she must be dreaming, but she clearly heard it. 'Open the door!' someone shouted. 'Open the door or we'll break it down!'

It was her husband's voice, hoarse with an excitement she had never heard in it before. At first, her horror robbed her of speech, as often happens in a dream, but at last she found her voice again. 'Don't!' she screamed, clinging to Toni. 'Don't open the door! For God's sake, don't!'

But Toni pushed her away. In his blue silk pyjamas, he tore himself from the frantic Elisabeth and hurried to the door. She sprang after him, in her shift, with her feet bare and her hair loose. The door flew open, and there stood the Professor, with an unknown man by his side. Elisabeth began to scream. The Professor's whole body shook. 'You wretch!' he rasped. 'You miserable wretch!' He rushed at her and would have struck her, but Toni and the unknown man held him fast by the arms.

Elisabeth listened with half an ear to her husband's invective, which seemed to flood over her. Why am I here? she thought. What am I doing here? She had wrapped the bedspread tightly around herself because she was particularly embarrassed in front of the unknown man. He just stood there, calmly, almost expertly, taking stock of the room, examining Elisabeth in her state of undress and Toni, who had retreated into a window recess. When he saw that the Professor was so worked up that he could hardly stand, he patted him genially on the shoulder. 'That'll do,' he said. 'What more do you need?'

The Professor looked up and mopped the sweat from his brow. 'You're right,' he said, 'there's nothing more to be done. You go to your sister,' he said to Elisabeth. 'You'll be hearing from my lawyer. He'll draw up all the necessary papers.'

Then he turned as if to launch himself at Toni, but the unknown man whispered something in his ear. With a gesture of disgust, the Professor turned away and they left.

Elisabeth stared after them, as if it was all a dream. The unbelievable horror of everything that had happened still did not feel quite real. She did not even ask herself any questions. Such as how the Professor had come to be there or who the unknown man was, or why Toni's behaviour had been so passive. In fact, it was as if Toni had been completely deleted from her mind.

At last he turned to her, more in compassion than in agitation or shock. 'Come on,' he said, 'get dressed. You can't stay here. I'll take you to your sister's.'

For the first time that day, he was kind to her, helped her get dressed, spoke to her gently. But Elisabeth scarcely noticed, she was sunk in a state of torpor.

Toni took her to her sister's. 'I'll come tomorrow,' he promised. 'Then we'll work out what to do.'

Mechanically, Elisabeth climbed the stairs, returned the concierge's greeting, rang the bell. No one answered. Then Elisabeth remembered that yesterday—how infinitely long ago it seemed—her sister had mentioned that she was going to the theatre. That meant she wouldn't be home before eleven. Elisabeth sat down on the stairs and waited. The lights in the house were all off, the door was locked; Elisabeth just sat and waited. And then, exhausted, she fell asleep.

She woke when her brother-in-law tripped over her on the stairs and her sister cried out in alarm. Elisabeth, sleepy and overtired as she was, gave such a confused account of herself that they thought at first that she had lost her mind. But when her sister finally understood, she burst into loud lamentations. What a disgrace! And such a fine, educated man as the Professor, too! She promised to keep Elisabeth with her for the night. But the next morning she would have to go back to her husband. There was nothing else to be done.

Very early in the morning, unbeknown to Elisabeth, her brother-in-law paid a visit to the Professor to initiate a reconciliation. But he returned disappointed. For the first— and perhaps the only—time in his life, the Professor had shown himself to be imperturbable. It was as if someone else's will was directing his own, thought the brother-in-law, who was otherwise not remotely addicted to psychology. The Professor didn't want to take Elisabeth back. Life with her had long been intolerable in any case. He had spoken to his lawyer and divorce proceedings had already begun. Elisabeth's small dowry was hers, of course, and he would add a little something of his own, even though it went against the grain. For the time being, Mizl would go to relatives of his, until he could find a better situation for the child. And that was the end of the ghastly mistake of his marriage.

After that, things began to move forward on uncannily well-oiled wheels. Elisabeth felt as if she had been caught up in the cogs of a machine that had been sent to crush her. She didn't think; she didn't feel; she just did as she was told. She, too, engaged a lawyer, but there wasn't much of a case. It was all completely clear. And Toni didn't appear.

The day after, he had sent her a letter and a large bunch of flowers. The letter said that unfortunately he had been unexpectedly called away but would soon be back. He went on with words of comfort. She had been unlucky so far but life still had plenty to offer. Then the days went by and he never came. Elisabeth was not at all surprised that he did not come. She had always known that this was not love.

The other sister, the wife of the textile merchant from Linz, had also come, and the sisters sat over innumerable cups of coffee, discussing what should be done about Elisabeth. Although both were good-natured and keen to help, the whole business gave them a frisson of the kind of thrill that they craved. Elisabeth had always been the prettiest of the three and had made the best match—socially, if not materially. So they were nothing loth to offer their help to the Professor's wife. Above all, they insisted that Toni must be contacted. Toni was the one who was to blame for all this; he couldn't be allowed to make a convenient escape. Elisabeth was reluctant at first. But she couldn't just turn a blind eye to her sisters' judgement. She didn't love Toni but her vanity was deeply wounded. So she went to him.

She rang the bell but nobody answered. She found the caretaker and asked if Mr Anton Brückler was at home.

'Who?' the caretaker said. 'No one of that name here.'

'But there must be,' Elisabeth insisted. 'I once visited him here myself.'

The caretaker shrugged. 'Well, after all, Miss, this is a lodging house, it goes on monthly lets. I mean, if you expect me to know all of the gentlemen…'

'But you *must* know him,' Elisabeth urged, describing him: medium height, dark moustache, strikingly pale eyes.

The woman now remembered. 'Oh, I know. He took the room for a month from the first of May. Someone else moved in in June.'

The first of May. And she had first seen him on the second of May.

The caretaker tried to comfort her. 'There, there, all men are the same, yours is no exception! Every now and then a lady comes to ask about one of the gentlemen who live here. And we can never give any information. Not one of the gentlemen has ever given us his real name.'

Elisabeth went away disheartened. She remembered that Toni had said he was a civil servant and so she went to the ministries to enquire. There had never been anyone by that name on their books. She looked in the address book and found several Brücklers: a butcher, an accountant, a shop assistant. She went to see each of them in turn, but of course none of them was called Anton, nor did any of them have a relative by that name. But the shop assistant, who quickly understood the situation, offered to take his namesake's place.

Elisabeth now knew that she had been well and truly duped and abandoned.

She wasn't anxious on account of her child but she was afraid to meet her daughter's eyes and of the questions she would ask, and was glad that she didn't need to see her for a while. The hateful moment when the divorce was pronounced, and she saw her husband face to face, albeit from a distance, left her cold. All feeling in her was completely paralysed and she, who had always been so bright and active, now sat idle for days on end.

And yet, had she been able to reflect clearly on what had happened, she would have realised that it caused her no pain. It was more that her whole being rebelled against the idea that she, who had been so eminently suited to the kind of life she had led, had now been torn from it, expelled from the ranks of the bourgeoisie and thrust into a new and hostile kind of existence that was completely alien to her nature.

And why? Because someone had happened to look at her in the street.

But no, the cause lay deeper than that: it was because she had married a man who was separated from her by a yawning spiritual gulf. A man she now realised she no longer loved. Why wasn't he happy with me, simple and dutiful as I was? she asked herself resentfully. Why didn't he love me for the things I could offer him? Is a good and dutiful wife worth so little? Sometimes it occurred to her to wonder whether she had not also been partially to blame for their marital discord, whether she hadn't got on his nerves. But she quickly dismissed such thoughts. It felt more comfortable to cast herself as the victim.

She told herself that she was going to have to find something to do. She could not stay with her sister forever; her sister lived in rather straitened circumstances and had a very cramped flat. Even if she paid a little towards her keep and saved her sister the expense of a maid, she and her husband had got so used to being by themselves that they could not but find the presence of a third person irksome. Elisabeth would have preferred to go to the other sister in Linz, but what would a small, pious town like that make of a divorcee?

And then, a few months later, something happened to give her a jolt and provide her with the courage to face life again. She bumped into Mali, her former maid, at the market. Although Mali had always tended to be on a war footing with the Professor's wife, she now rushed up to her former mistress and excitedly filled her in on all the latest developments. She was no longer working for the Professor; Madame Stefani had shown her the door. The Professor wanted to marry Madame Stefani and to that end had applied for Hungarian citizenship. Well, Madame Stefani might be clever but she was an awful tyrant. She never consulted him; it was she who made all the decisions and he just went along with everything as if he didn't have a mind of his own. From this, Mali went on to talk about her current employer, who was a dragon. Elisabeth was invited to imagine being asked to bring home a kilo of rump steak for eighty *kreuzers*, when every fool knew that such a thing was no longer to be had. And on it went.

Elisabeth listened. She even listened with interest to what Mali was saying about her new employer. Suddenly she felt as if something had fallen away from her, something that had been keeping her down. The Professor had come to terms with his fate; now she had to do the same. Suddenly, she felt completely free, like someone who has been allowed to begin a new life with a clear conscience. She still had plenty of unspent energy, plenty of life still lay before her. She said goodbye to Mali, sat down on a bench and began to think.

She couldn't live off the interest on her own money. But neither did she want to. She needed to work; she would have to look for something. Of course, she hadn't had much training but she had a good head for domestic economy and would put that to good use. As if impelled by a new resolve, she went straight to an employment agency and placed an advertisement.

Her sister and brother-in-law were delighted at the prospect of her standing on her own two feet, and for a few days Elisabeth was happy. Of course, the kind of job she was looking for was not easy to find. The people looking for housekeepers were mostly widows, or single men who assessed her appearance with rather too complacent smiles, and for the time being Elisabeth wanted nothing to do with men.

Finally, after a long search, she found what she wanted. A baroness was looking for a housekeeper on her estate. Experience was less important to her than complete honesty and common sense. She took to Elisabeth at first sight. What expertise she lacked, she would soon able to acquire, since the current housekeeper, who was getting married in a few months, would be able to train her. Elisabeth was to start work in just eight days. The estate was in Styria, where it was peaceful and beautiful.

Elisabeth parted from the friendly baroness in high spirits. Life seemed to be full of promise once more. She wanted to get away from the noise and clamour of the city; she longed to be amidst nature, somewhere where she could work and forget. She felt that she would become pure again, pure and clean. Perhaps she would once again have something to offer to her child, would earn the right to reclaim her. And perhaps she would find happiness, too. Involuntarily she stretched out her arms, her firm, white, muscular arms, arms made for labour and for earthy female embraces. A vision rose before her of a healthy, strong, doughty life with some man, a forester or a local steward, a life lived among fields and cattle, a life of busy weekdays and quiet Sundays sitting cosily over coffee and cakes and then strolling peacefully in the woods, where it smelled of damp leaves. That was the kind of life she craved; the kind of life she had been brought up for, the kind of life which suited her intellectual range.

The time it took her to paint this image was the last happy minute of Elisabeth's life.

Because suddenly she froze. A man brushed hastily past her. She recognised him. It was Toni. It seemed that he recognised her, too, although he gave no sign of it, but hurried on his way. An inner voice urged Elisabeth to do the same: Pretend you don't know him! It's for your own good! But she ignored it. A surge of red-hot anger flared up in her, fury against the man who had betrayed her. At the very least, she wanted to hurl her contempt in his face. She ran after him; he ran faster. It turned into a chase. The man ducked into a side street but a lorry blocked his way. Elisabeth grabbed him by the sleeve.

'Let me go,' he groaned, turning pale.

'You stay right where you are!' Elisabeth ground out, her anger making her voice ugly. She pulled him into an entranceway. 'Why did you do what you did?' she hissed.

'Let me go!' he pleaded. 'Let me go!'

'You're not going anywhere!' cried Elisabeth, clawing at him. 'I'll call the police. You'll pay for this!'

'Calling the police won't do any good,' said Toni, almost with a smile. 'I beg you, let me go. I feel for you, poor fool. But let me go. Believe me, it's better for you to let me go.'

'Not until you've at least told me your real name,' Elisabeth insisted. 'Everything about you was a lie, even your name.'

Toni tried to break free, but Elisabeth was beside herself.

'I'll strangle you if you don't talk,' she told him, putting her hands around his throat.

He tried to fight her off but he felt himself turning blue in the face and suddenly he knew that he was in danger.

'Talk,' she spat, 'talk!'

He made a laboured gesture, signalling that he was willing to do so. She loosened her grip but still did not let him go.

'Ask the Minotaur Detective Agency who I am,' he croaked.

'What do you mean?' she asked.

'Just go and as them!'

Once more, she tightened her grip. 'Talk sense!'

'Very well,' he said. 'I was hired by Madame Stefani to seduce you, so that your husband could get rid of you, since he lacked the initiative to divorce you without good reason.'

At that, Elisabeth released him completely. It was her turn to go pale. She still didn't quite understand him.

'It's true,' he went on. 'There are people whose business

this is. I specialise in adultery. It's not a very noble business, but what's a former army officer who has no other skills supposed to do? You become a detective, that's what you do. There's more suffering in life than you might think. And plenty of women have made themselves very happy by ridding themselves of their odious husbands. I felt sorry for you at first. I advised you let your husband go. A woman like Edith Stefani knows no mercy. But you wouldn't hear of it. And when I went to see her that evening—because I reported to her every day—she said, 'In that case, we will have to resort to desperate measures.' You must admit that everything was cleverly planned. As soon as you left home, your unsuspecting husband received an anonymous letter informing him of your infidelity. A witness was also produced. I was afraid that he would get there before you, because you arrived so late. Well, now you know everything,' Toni said, suddenly friendly. 'Poor dupe, it would be better if you didn't! But after all, a pretty little lady like you…'

He made as if to lean towards her but she shoved him in the stomach. He saw a dangerous glint in her eyes and elected to make himself scarce.

She didn't lift a hand to stop him. She stood leaning against the wall for a while, then went on her way. Not broken, not cast down, but standing erect, like someone who knows exactly what they want to do. As she walked, she looked closely at all the shops. She found a chemist's that was still open. She went in.

Then she went and waited in the Professor's entranceway. It didn't take long. A lady appeared.

Then a terrible scream rang out.

People rushed to see what had happened and found a woman lying unconscious on the ground with her eyes burnt out. Then they turned and flung themselves at Elisabeth, who was trying to escape. She struggled but they held her fast. A whisper of 'Vitriol' went round the little gaggle. Then the voices got louder and louder. And suddenly, out of nowhere, a reporter was at the scene, scribbling in a notepad:

'Revenge attack. The first wife of Professor X, divorced through her own guilty conduct, has today made an attempt on the life of the Professor's future new bride…'

Then a cry of 'Police!' went up and the crowd parted respectfully on either side to let them through.

And the tide of life surged over Elisabeth and sucked her under.

Die Spießbürgerin. 1914

Joseph Roth

SOMETHING EVER RARER

It is something ever rarer, in this age of self-evident facts and foregone conclusions, to come across the kinds of remarkable coincidence which—if one believes what one is told—one used to encounter on an almost daily basis. Yet even today, by those who make people and their destinies their careful study, examples of such chains of events can be found, events that appear to have been shaped not by some blind will but by a kind of poetic power that seems from time to time to guide the world's affairs.

Of all the people I have ever come across, there is probably no one who has had such a strange, tragi-comic, random-yet-inevitable fate as the man I am about to describe and whose surname I deliberately withhold—not because he still numbers among my acquaintance but because I am certain that more twists and turns of outrageous fortune still lie before him, and by baldly stating a bald fact, I fear that I might pervert their course.

On the 3rd of November 1918, Heinrich P. took the decision to earn his daily bread by becoming a writer.

This was in the early days of the Revolution, a time when people still believed that, although as individuals they could have no possible influence on the grand course of events, yet in certain ways they might still have some connection to them.

Like so many million others, Heinrich P. had gone to war, and—like so very few—had returned home safe and well. As an officer in the Austro-Hungarian Army he had, with the disintegration of the Empire, suddenly found himself a civilian citizen of the new Czech state.

On the 1st of November 1918 he returned to Brünn[14], the city of his birth. Everything he saw there—the Revolution being waged in one of the capitals of the erstwhile Crown Lands; the marching of the military band, still dressed in their imperial uniforms but playing a brand new national anthem; the gangs of Czechs who went around tearing the old cockades from the officers' caps; the foolish glee of the freshly liberated nation—all of this seemed to Heinrich P. to cry out for literary expression, and thus for a pen to do the expressing. Passive though he naturally was, Heinrich P. viewed the Revolution through the lens of historical perspective. He told himself that he was 'studying events'; and the swiftness and magnitude of everything that happened left him no time to worry about his own fate or the foreseeable future. Purely because all the other recently returned officers were also doing it, he went one morning to the Army HQ, where the official language was now Czech—that second, regional tongue that came almost as easily to them all as their own native German. There he was told that the new government had a place for him in the new army, which needed officers. Saying that he wanted some time to think it over, he took his previous month's pay packet and asked for permission to go to Prague. Then he went to the station, boarded the train and searched—through force of habit—for a seat in a second-class compartment, whereupon he realised that the whole train was made up of third-class carriages. Accordingly, he took a seat on one of the rows of hard wooden benches, most of which were occupied by troops.

During the journey, he made the acquaintance of one of those swift and impromptu stop-and-search parties that, in the first flushes of revolutionary zeal, wanting to make themselves unnecessarily useful, had got into the habit of searching trains in which there was nothing at all to find. And it was as if it had taken this stop-and-search party in their Czech Sokol uniforms to remind Heinrich P. of the new order of things; as if this clear and unambiguous change in outward appearances had alerted him to the change in his own personal circumstances. Because only now did Heinrich P. begin to think about his foreseeable future and to occupy his mind with those material considerations which must slowly and surely begin to pose an existential threat.

He still had a bit of money. He had managed to save a couple of thousand Marks from his officer's pay. But now he began to reproach himself for not accepting the offer to join the new army. What, after all, was a man of his passive nature to do in these vociferously active times? He was, he felt, just loitering on the periphery of events, not penetrating the heart of things. He was as far from being able to influence those things as they were from being able to affect him. Assuming, of course, that he had the talent to describe them, he wanted to try to approach them from the perspective that only a writer knows how to find, but—did he have the ability to write? He remembered the headmaster of his grammar school, who used to write theatre reviews for the local newspaper. Was old Von Hauer still alive, he wondered? Heinrich P. arrived in Prague, was stopped by a platoon of soldiers, suffered them to check his papers, and was genuinely delighted to recognise, in the head of the new platoon, the old janitor from his grammar school. He went to see his aunt.

She belonged to that class of relative for whom a reunion with a male member of the family gives rise in equal measure to joyful enthusiasm and to lamentations over the desperate state of the times. Heinrich P. gave her the money for which she claimed to have a desperately pressing need, then took himself into the city. He went to look up his old headmaster, Von Hauer, and celebrated a reunion with him that once again partook of equal parts of personal joy and political woe at the sudden and complete reversal of fortunes. Von Hauer gave him a letter of introduction to the editor of the local paper. It was to this paper that Heinrich delivered an account of his revolutionary experiences. The article appeared the following day and it seemed to Heinrich, when he read it, as if he had simply invented it all: the Revolution, the return home, the goings-on at the railway station. He began to doubt himself. He felt that he had overdone both the zeal and the confusion and that between the reality of that Revolution and his portrayal of it yawned a gulf of difference as wide as that between the Revolution and the War. He had written of intoxication and drunkenness; but the fact was, that he had seen no more men under the influence than one normally sees on an ordinary Sunday afternoon in peacetime.

As he was still mulling over these things, a man came to see him, saying that he was a detective and claiming to have orders to take him to a certain Dr Slama at Police HQ. Dr Slama turned out to be the new government censor. He said that he had been wanting to make Heinrich P.'s acquaintance and hoped that he might possibly be able to tempt him—talented with the pen as he so clearly was—to work for the Czech government, just as Mr Slama himself, a former official of the Empire, had likewise been tempted.

The temptation to devote himself to the cause of the new Czech Republic, however, was one that Heinrich P. was able to resist. This was not because Heinrich P. was a committed believer in the German nation but owed more to the fact that, his character being what it was, he was determined to avoid any situation which would require him to act. If he had, in fact, taken the trouble to think about the current plight of the German portion of the population, he would have come to the conclusion that what he knew of it seemed fully aligned with his predisposition for passivity. But at that point, Heinrich P. was not thinking very much at all. His own situation—like that of the population in general—seemed far more complicated than was necessary. Lover of quiet that he was, he decided to go to one of those peaceable countries where political conflicts seem to have been put aside centuries ago and where perpetual concord is granted to the lucky denizens.

And so, with what remained of his money, he took himself to Switzerland, pitched temporary camp in Zurich and, from a sense that one is duty-bound do *something*, began writing articles for German newspapers. His income remained meagre, his expenses began nibbling into his savings, until one day, around June of 1919, he realised that he could not pay his rent.

It is clear, however, that a merciful-unmerciful Providence watches over certain young men, and that however banal its methods might seem, its favourites nevertheless manage to stagger on a little longer, shielded from the kind of premature calamities that would make stories like this one impossible to tell. Banal as this Providence might be, so also is the coincidence that Heinrich P.'s landlady happened to have a niece and that this niece came to live in the building where Heinrich lodged, and that the elderly lady became possessed with the natural desire that her niece should make her only lodger's near acquaintance. How easily such a banal circumstance can turn into a fatality for the gentleman concerned, the reader is doubtless well aware, and thus we are absolved of having to describe how Heinrich P. was duped into falling in love and how it was pure instinct that permitted him to flee the clutches of bourgeois life. Rather, we content ourselves with the sudden arrival of a letter, addressed to Heinrich and which read as follows:

My dear friend,
A short while ago I had the good fortune to spot your name in a newspaper and was reminded of the weeks and months we spent together in the field. After the collapse of the Empire I moved to Germany, where I now live, in Berlin. I am a lawyer, I have married (advantageously) and am one of the legal advisors in my father-in-law's firm. It was not without astonishment that I learned that you live in

Zurich—and a certain wistfulness came over me, which, laughable though you may find it, has prompted me to write. My wife and I will be going to Marseilles next week and would be very happy if you could join us. Send us a wire if you are able to meet us at Basel station at 2 o'clock in the afternoon on the 28th of July.

Your friend,
Otto Reichhardt

Immer seltener werden in dieser Welt. Undated

Kálmán Mikszáth

LŐRINC'S HATS

'I say, Larry,' I said one day, sitting myself down beside my friend Lőrinc, who was reading *Le Figaro* at the Danube Kiosk[15]. 'Where did you get that splendid hat?'

The unsuspecting fellow put down his newspaper, took off his hat and looked inside it. 'I bought it in Kolozsvár[16],' he said. 'Not bad, is it?'

'How much d'you want for it?'

My friend went back to his *Figaro* and limited himself to saying, rather stiffly, 'I'll get them to send you one.' And with that he continued reading his newspaper.

'No, no, no!' I insisted. 'I really like the simple, elegant style of *that* hat. I've simply got to have *that* one.'

'You can't go around wearing a hand-me-down hat! Give me your head measurements and I'll write to the hat-maker today. What do you say to that?'

'It absolutely won't do at all. That hat of yours has developed a few snags and wrinkles. One can't just duplicate a thing like that. The fact that it's a tiny bit worn is just the thing I love about it. *Do* let me have it, Larry, there's a good fellow! It would make me *so* happy…'

And I pestered him and pestered him so mercilessly that eventually, he got fed up.

'For Heaven's sake!' he said, a little irritably. 'It's quite obvious that you aren't going to let me read my newspaper in peace. Very well, then, I'll give you the hat. On one condition…'

'Anything, at your service!'

'That you buy me another one to replace it.'

So off we went to Skrivan's[17] and Larry chose a wide-brimmed grey hat with a white band. Or rather, he didn't exactly *choose* it; he just settled for the first thing that was the right size. There is nothing—but nothing—in Lőrinc's character that could be termed vain. In fact, it must be said that he is rather an ill-favoured fellow. He pays no attention at all to what he wears and he has never had much of an eye for the ladies. But perhaps that has more to do with the fact that no lady has ever had much of an eye for him, either. (I should add that this assessment was made before the episode of the Kolozsvár hat.)

The next day, I found him sitting at his usual table, under the grey hat from Skriván's, reading *Le Figaro*. An impish little idea crossed my mind. Human nature is ungrateful, I am sorry to say, and perennially prone to mischief. I discussed my idea with Paul Szabó—who is always up for a prank—and, fully primed, he sat himself down at Larry's side.

'What are you so engrossed in?'

'I'm reading *Le Figaro*,' said Lőrinc, without looking up from his newspaper.

'By Jove, that's a smashing hat you've got!'

'I beg your pardon?' stammered Larry, rather taken aback.

'Your hat. Where did you get it?'

With visible annoyance, Larry threw down his newspaper

and turned suspicious eyes on Paul.

'My hat? Are you asking about my hat? Why is my hat so interesting all of a sudden?'

For a man who was normally so mild-mannered, he sounded positively fierce.

'I mean, is a man's hat to prevent him from reading his newspaper?' he burst out angrily. 'What is the meaning of this sudden to-do about my hats? What do you want?'

'Oh, come now, old friend!' said Paul soothingly. 'What's got into you? Have I hurt your feelings? Have I said something wrong?'

'I just want to know why my hat bothers you so much.'

'*Bothers* me? But on the contrary—I was singing its praises. I've never seen such a fine hat. The epitome of chic. It has a genuine *je ne sais quoi*.'

'For Heaven's sake!' cried Larry, throwing his hat down disbelievingly on the marble tabletop. 'There are thousands of hats like this at Skriván's.'

'I tell you what, Larry. Why don't you let me have it?'

'Now just stop it, I tell you! You'll get me riled. Haven't I told you that there are thousands of hats like this at Skriván's? Why can't you go to Skriván's yourself?'

'You don't understand, Larry. It's these little snags and wrinkles… They are what make it, I swear. That little kink in the brim. The shape of the dent in the crown.'

'Oh, have done with you! What a lot of old rot!'

'Be a sport, Larry. Don't deny me this little request. I beg you, as a friend.'

'Just go to Skriván's!'

'Please, Larry old thing,' begged Paul wickedly. 'I'll take you to Pórfi's[18] in exchange and buy you the very finest hat they have.'

'Oh, very well,' grumbled the owner of the marvellous hats. 'I'll come with you. I'll go along with it one more time. But enough is enough, you know. I'll only do it this once.'

And as if to underline his meaning, his raised his fists menacingly.

So off they went. And the next day, Larry was seen sitting by the burbling fountain, under the dwarf acacia tree, wearing a black pork-pie hat.

This time, in order to pursue our little jape, Paul and I needed to find another accomplice. We found just the person, in the form of Max Ocskoványi. He is a bit of a feeble fellow, always willing to be used as a 'useful idiot'. All Paul Szabó needed to tell him was that Larry was fanatical about swapping hats and that nothing pleased him better than hearing people admiring his headgear.

'Good morning, Sir,' said the hapless Ocskoványi. 'May I…?' And he drew up a chair next to Lőrinc's. 'How do you do? Waiter—a cappuccino! Did you have a pleasant summer? Where did you spend it?'

'Nowhere,' came the muttered answer.

Lőrinc, to be honest, was behaving rather peculiarly. He was nodding and smiling to all the ladies that passed by, in a way that was very far from being his custom. He barely cast a glance at his *Figaro*.

'Scorching weather, we're having, isn't it?' Ocskoványi went on, mopping his heated brow.

'Mm—yes, it is rather,' said Lőrinc, by now a little peevish, his voice more resembling his normal gruff tone.

'But I say! What a spanking hat you've got…'

Instantly, the blood flew to Larry's face. He jumped to his feet like a stricken boar.

'Sir!' he thundered. 'What, may I ask, has my hat to do with you?'

'I…nothing!' stuttered Ocskoványi, turning pale. 'I—I was just wondering if—if I might acquire it from you…'

'Acquire it? You as well!' cried Lőrinc, with a splutter. 'Am I going to have to go into exile from my own country because of these dratted hats of mine? What on earth is going on? Eh? What's all this about?' He waved his arms in the air, wildly gesticulating and swearing colourfully. His nostrils had started quivering like a pair of blacksmith's bellows. 'Am I to go about hatless from now on? Mm? Are you going to force me to retreat into the woods like a hunted stag, cowering away where I can't be seen?'

Poor Max Ocskoványi sat rooted to the spot like a pillar of salt. He had no idea what had brought this on.

'But my dear Sir, I beg you, please…!'

'No buts and no begging!' A stream of invective began to pour from Larry's mouth. 'You're a very stupid, vain young man, there are no two ways about it!'

'Sir, I beg you, restrain yourself!'

'Restrain? I certainly shall not restrain myself. You're a very foolish, vain young madman.'

'But…'

'But nothing! I'll have you know, young whippersnapper…'

And as he said this, Lőrinc's habitually rather mildew-coloured, awkward-featured face took on an expression of desperate fury and his eyes began to bulge in their sockets, '…I'll have you know that you are not the first man of your ilk to accost me. Let me tell you…'

'Tell me what?'

Larry seemed to have regained control of himself by this time. His grey eyes began to twitch. He was aware that his intemperate shouting and gesticulating had attracted the attention of all the nearby tables. As if to call a truce, he placed a large, hirsute hand over his mouth, and then said, *sotto voce*,

'I'll have you know, young man, that this hat you see me in now is the *third* hat I have worn in as many days.'

'Indeed!'

'I'm sure you know George Pélyi? Well, the day before yesterday, he saw me wearing a certain hat and bothered me and bothered me until I sold it to him. The poor fool was under the impression that it would cut the same dash on *his* head as it had on mine. But have you seen him in it? I mean, he looks a perfect fright! But never mind, I let him have it. He bought me a replacement from Skriván's for four forints. But what do you think happens next? I'll tell you what happens next. Paul Szabó sees the Skriván hat—this was yesterday—and goes absolutely mad for it. He coaxes and wheedles until I finally let him have it. And today it's *you* who has descended on me, badgering me about my hat…'

'I had no idea, Sir. Forgive me. I give you my word, I had no idea…' babbled the unfortunate Max.

'Well, now you know, young man. And be advised by me, don't go throwing your money away out of vanity. After all, there are hundreds of hats like this at Skriván's. Or at Þórfi's. They are all precisely the same, you can take my word for it. I mean, every man in town has got a hat like mine. But don't be under any illusion. The only reason they seem so fine to you is because of the way I wear them.'

And from that day forward, Lőrinc was a changed man. Once so modest, so undemanding and so punctilious, he has now taken to strutting up and down Váci Street[19], looking at himself almost flirtatiously in all the shop windows. Every week he buys himself a new hat and sports it with a studied air, as if to advertise it to all the passers-by. 'I say, ladies and gentlemen, d'you see this rather wonderful hat I'm wearing?'

We see it. Indeed we do. But not on Larry's head. Because scores and scores of people are wearing hats like that. In literature. In politics. And in other places.

A Lőrinc kalapjai. 1886

Elek Gozsdu

AUTUMN RAIN

Her name was Lily and today was her fortieth birthday. In her mind, the prospect of being forty had always seemed something so remote and far away in the future that she had come to view it as an age she would never actually attain. And as a result, she had always been merry and light-hearted. Until now.

Apart from her lean-bodied, silver-headed husband, there were few people who knew when her birthday was. And in her broad good humour and perpetual whirl of social engagements, Lily sometimes even forgot it herself.

It was a damp, dreary October day. The meet had been called off. From the window of her little sitting-room, Lily watched the steady stream of raindrops falling onto the slates of the roof opposite, heard the monotonous gurgling sound that the rainwater made as it flowed along the gutter. The tiny patch of sky that she could see beyond the heavy silk drapes was uniformly grey and the drizzle fell from it relentlessly, in a ceaseless stream. She peered out at the street and watched the people scurrying up and down the glistening tarmac, their necks hunched into their collars, cold and wet beneath their dripping umbrellas.

Wet, cold, miserable autumn day!

Dejected and depressed, Lily sank back onto her brightly

upholstered little divan. She had a sensation of something lying particularly heavily on her heart. She felt perilously close to tears.

She was expecting no visitors. She would spend the whole day on her own. The whole day.

Unusually for her, she was wearing neither rouge nor powder. She had not crimped her hair and she had chosen a plain black dress. Her only concession to vanity was the white fall of frothy lace which adorned her throat and bosom.

She looked interesting—even beautiful—in the unlit room. Her brown hair was still lustrous, her black eyes still bright. And there were occasions when, mounted on her black hunter, tearing along at a gallop, the contours of her slender waist still gave her the appearance of a young girl. Only her hands, less plump than formerly, betrayed her age a little; her hands and the tiny fine lines on her forehead. But one soon forgot those tiny lines when one saw her shining eyes.

Wet, cold, miserable autumn day!

It occurred to Lily that one day—and in the not-too-distant future, too—she would be spending all her days alone, the sunny ones as well as the wet and dismal. She had no children. There were only her women friends to fall back on. Oh, those women friends!

She felt a burning, keenly painful desire for something she couldn't have. She felt bitter and dissatisfied. She was fed up with the rain and began to ask herself why she had ever been born, if all that was going to happen was this endless, remorseless, monotonous rain, rain, rain. She felt that she loved no one and that no one loved her.

There was a time, not very long ago, when the sun had shone warm and benignly; when all the flowers had been in bloom and bursting with perfume and such thoughts had never entered her head. She had believed she loved everyone and that everyone loved her. There had been no cold, remorseless rain in those days. But that was a long time ago.

How had she even come to marry Géza? Oh, yes, now she remembered. They had been doing a charity event at the stables, for orphan children. There had been twenty of them, decked out in fancy Rococo costumes. The day of the dress rehearsal had been a cold, foggy, gloomy autumn day as well. That was when she had met Géza.

Géza had been a good-looking young man. Good-natured, too. They had begun to go riding together. They had fallen in love. They got married in the spring. And they still loved each other. Why would they not? Lily knew that Géza had strayed elsewhere, enjoyed a little dalliance from time to time; but if it amused him to do so—well, why on earth not?

Lily had always been faithful. And today, in this dismal, rainy weather, she felt that she had done the right thing.

The summer was over. It had not been a hot one. It had been mild and pleasant and cool. No thunderstorms. Nothing special. A summer full of harmless little pleasures. A fine mount. A fox taken. A pretty dress. The company of amiable gentlemen and ladies. A nicely put-together dinner. It was all one needed. And thus she had reached her fortieth birthday.

And she felt that she loved no one and that no one loved her.

If only she had children, or at least a child!

The cold autumn rain was still falling. The people were still scurrying to and fro under their sodden umbrellas.

If she had a child, she wouldn't be alone. She wouldn't dread cold autumn days like this one, days when the meet was cancelled and she couldn't go fox-hunting.

Why did the rain go on and on? Why had she no children?

Lily felt completely alone in a vast universe, connected to no one and interested in nothing. She felt like a guest in her own beautiful, palatially appointed home. She found it ridiculous how seriously she and Géza took their position in the world, their place in society, the roles they sought to play in it. It occurred to her that she and Géza no longer had anything to say to one another. If ever she found herself alone with him, she tried to peel back the layers to reveal the Géza she used to know, the man at whose side she had ridden, that first day at the stables. Because the face he always presented to the world, that affable, jocular but ultimately unknowable Géza, was a stranger to her. He was not unpleasant to live with. He was a good partner in that respect. But really, they had nothing in common.

Those were the thoughts that chased across Lily's mind that gloomy, rainy autumn afternoon.

If only she had a child!

Lily realised that she was cold. She began pacing briskly up and down the room. An idea took hold of her that suddenly wouldn't let her go. She couldn't rid herself of the bitterness, of the reproaches it conjured up. What is the point of riches? she asked herself. And what was the point of all her finery if she was so utterly alone?

While she was restlessly pacing up and down, the door silently opened; and when she turned round, there was Géza.

'Good evening, Lily!' He held out both hands in friendly greeting. 'Aren't we going to the theatre?'

His arrival had taken Lily by surprise. For a while, she couldn't find her voice.

'Well? Are we going or aren't we?'

Lily sat down in front of the fire. 'No,' she said. 'I'm not in the mood.'

'Hallelujah! It will be nice to stay at home for once.'

Géza took a seat opposite her.

'Why today, in particular?' Lily asked. 'Could it be because it's my fortieth birthday?'

'Are you really forty, Lily darling? You *can't* be, I don't believe it!'

'Don't make fun of me, Géza. It's not fair.'

'I'm sorry. Give me your hand. There—that's better. You know, Lily my dear, we really ought to spend more time together.'

'Haven't we seen enough of each other? We know each other inside out, don't we? But it's still not enough to see us through a lifetime.'

'Not enough, Lily?'

'Not if we're the main focus of each other's lives, no.'

'Are you saying you're tired of me?'

'Are you pretending you aren't tired of *me*?'

'Yes! I mean, no! I'm *not* tired of you, Lily!'

'Well, I suppose it stands to reason. You only seek me out when you feel like it or when you've nothing better to do.'

'Lily!'

'When you're sick of your horses and your guns. When the gaming tables feel like a dead bore and when you decide that, of all your female acquaintance, it's your wife who's the least artificial after all. Isn't that the same as being tired of me?'

'I do believe you're jealous!'

'I'm not jealous in the least,' Lily retorted. 'I'm not and I never have been. But I am very alone. I have no one to love and no one who loves me. I'm alone and I always will be…'

'But Lily, for pity's sake! You've always seemed so contented, so satisfied. You've been able to amuse yourself exactly as you please. I've never once stood in your way. I've let you do precisely as you wish, always. I thought you were happy…'

'I feel so envious of women with children. I'm sick of married life, sick of you, sick of myself and sick of the whole world! Why was I born? How have I come to be forty all of a sudden? I don't want to get old. What for? Who is made happy because I exist? And whose existence makes *me* happy in return?'

'And you're making all this *my* fault?'

'Not only yours. It's mine as well. The idea of a joyless existence makes me shudder! Oh—I don't want to go on living!'

Lily fell silent and stared into the fire. Géza listlessly lit a cigarette and stared in turn at the glowing coals. The room was sunk in a deep silence. The only sound was the autumn raindrops beating against the window and the water pouring from the gutter onto the pavement.

'Summer is over!' Lily murmured. 'And here we are on our own,' she added, her voice desolate.

'On our own, Lily!'

'On our own, Géza!' repeated Lily gloomily.

'Are you angry with me Lily?' Géza asked, not daring to meet her eye.

Lily made no answer.

'Forgive me, Lily. It's just—you see… I mean… Well, I didn't…'

'Perhaps, Géza. Perhaps. But then again, who knows…' said Lily quietly, as if talking to herself. With her eyes fixed on the ground, she fiddled with the lace at her throat.

Just then, the butler came in. On a finely wrought silver salver he proffered the plans for tomorrow's luncheon party.

Lily looked up. As if awakened from a reverie, she reached out and took the little gilt-edged card. As she began to read, her face became more and more animated. At last she cried,

'Geraldine was quite right! Paul is the finest chef in the Empire! A treasure—an absolute treasure! Look at this, Géza, dear! Just look at how this has been put together! It's a masterpiece!'

Géza pulled up a low pouffe and began to read:

'*Huitres d'Oste de…* Mature sherry… So far so good! *Consommé en tasse…* Oh no! No, no that won't do at all. Far too dull! What about *consommé tapioca aux oeufs* instead?'

'*Consommé tapioca aux oeufs*? Why, for heaven's sake?' snapped Lily, snatching the card from Géza's hand. 'I don't want that. I can't stand tapioca!'

'But just think for a minute, Lily. I mean, *aux oeufs*! To please me, Lily? Pretty please?' Géza wheedled.

'But why *aux oeufs*, precisely? I *loathe* eggs. No, it's a combination that won't do at all,' Lily said firmly.

'Not even to please me, my sweet? You know how partial I am to eggs! And after all…'

Lily laughed. 'Oh, very well, have it your way! *Consommé tapioca aux oeufs* it shall be. And to follow, *petites bouchées à la reine*! Agreed?'

'Absolutely!' nodded Géza, taking a puff of his cigarette.

'*Truites de rivière?*'

'Excellent!'

'*Filet de boeuf à la jardinière?*'

'Splendid!

'*Selle de chevreuil*? Compotes with Château Léoville?'

'Couldn't be better!'

'*Chapon de Styrie* with Steinberg Kabinett[20]?'

'Oh, Paul! I'd take you in my arms and kiss you if your nose weren't quite so red!'

'*Glace en forme, pâtisseries*, fruit, biscuits; Louis Roederer, liqueurs, coffee. There—we're done,' said Lily with satisfaction. Then, taking up a pen, she crossed out '*Consommé en tasse*' and in its place wrote '*Consommé tapioca aux oeufs*'. She tapped Géza's hand with the pen. 'There we are!' she said with a smile. 'Tell Paul that I am very satisfied,' she told the butler. 'Very satisfied indeed.'

The butler withdrew.

With a contented smile, Lily adjusted her lace, then rubbed her hands together. Her eyes shone as she said,

'I'm looking forward to tomorrow's luncheon. I'm looking forward to it very much!'

Géza leaned towards her and tenderly put his arm around her waist. Lily snuggled against him.

'You see, my Lily?' he said. 'There is always something worth living for. A menu like that does wonders to reconcile one to the ghastly business of life!'

'You're right,' Lily admitted softly.

They embraced. Then Lily asked eagerly,

'Will we go hunting tomorrow, do you think?'

But Géza just laughed and pointed at the window.

'D'you hear that? Listen!'

Endlessly, monotonously, the cold autumn rain continued to fall. Drip, drip, drip, as if it would never stop…

Őszi eső. 1892

Margit Kaffka

MADAM AND MISS

Dusk was falling when the woman came in, in a swift flurry of skirts. She took a deep breath. The air in the small shop was heavy with the scent of flowers. The girl, Tessa, was standing behind the cash desk sponging down the leaves of a large fan palm. She stepped out of the gloom, her plump figure, clad in its white smock, emerging quietly from behind the spiky green foliage. She held out both hands to her visitor, then drew her into an embrace.

'Good evening, ma'am! What a lovely scent of winter you've brought in from the street. I can smell it, clinging to the fur of your coat and stole.'

The air in the shop was distinctly close, artificially tropical. The young florist moved swiftly across the floor in her light, cambric smock. She retired with her visitor to the alcove, and without closing the door, left the shop in the hands of the elderly saleslady in the lace cap, who dealt silently and discreetly with the requests of all the customers: gentlemen on the way to the theatre or to an evening *soirée*, who had dropped in to purchase a nosegay of violets. The alcove, no more than a sliver of space beside the main shop, seemed as easy and relaxed as the girl herself. There was no atmosphere of secrecy there, no muffled words of regret or feigned light-heartedness.

'Nobody is on edge here,' the visitor remarked. 'The whole place seems to be asking, in mild surprise, why one can't just do away with all one's ruses and one's tortured pretexts.'

Hedwig, for that was the lady visitor's name, had said this once before, some time ago. She had said it while smilingly contemplating the plain, round, cast-iron wash-stand, with its cotton percale cloth patterned with large flowers. Now the two women were sitting opposite each other on a blue chenille divan, and Tessa was earnestly searching her visitor's face, a little like a doctor examining a patient. The lady looked pale, as if weighed down by a new onset of neuralgia. A kind of spasmodic stiffness seemed to play about her thin lips. The girl took her hand.

'So? Has something happened?'

'Oh, no! I mean, if it had…'

The lady bowed her head for a moment, and then the words burst from her in a sudden rush. Like someone walking across burning coals, as if ducking and weaving to escape her own tortuous thoughts, she launched into a confession.

'Nothing, no news. All I know is that he isn't being sent home from the mental hospital. They are keeping him there and the situation is hopeless. Oh Tessa, it's so awful! I can't get it out of my head—out of my heart. It's there all day long, morning, noon and night. And then the next day it starts all over again. And meanwhile one goes through the motions, one goes to the shops, one puts lunch on the table, one darns the children's stockings. Today, when it began to get dark, I just buried my head in my hands and began contemplating that inner blackness which seems to fill my soul—and then before

I knew it, the children had come home from school and they thought I was crying or that I was in some sort of physical pain and they threw themselves into my arms. Oh, bless them! But I just pushed them away. I shook them off as if they were some kind of ghastly cross one is expected to bear. A burden from which there is no escape. And then I was appalled at myself and came running to you. Oh, Tessa! Say something!'

Comfortingly, the girl stroked the other woman's gloved hand with her white, sturdy fingers. Her eyes contained a kind of soothing light, a light suffused with a naïve belief in its power to console. Simply and quietly, she said,

'If only he had died, poor fellow!'

Her words were completely sincere; they came from the bottom of her heart. But her reward from the other the woman was a look of outrage.

'Why do you talk like that, as if there were no hope? Do you really think it's too late?'

'You know it's too late, Hedda. Why didn't you listen to me before?'

For some time, the other woman said nothing. Then she spoke.

'Up to now, you have always been on my side. You've been encouraging, you've tried to help. But are you now saying you think it would have been wrong? A sin, I mean?'

'I don't know. I haven't really thought about it. I saw that you were unhappy, I saw that you were struggling, and I thought it was because of your situation. And so I thought, very well, be happy, then. Break free, tear it all down, see if it helps. I compared your position with mine. I remembered the day I left everything behind. My home town, my job, the fiancé who had lied to me. I hated Budapest when I first got here. I had had a secure position in a well-respected school and my trousseau was ready and waiting. But I didn't regret my decision, even if only because it was what I'd made up my mind to do. I mean, I would have had to compromise a good deal if I'd married my fiancé. And I'd have ended up with just as many good days and just as many bad ones as I have now. It honestly makes no difference. But of course, you aren't like me. You've made yourself unhappy on purpose, because it suits you to be that way.'

'How can you talk like that? Do you think this is all just the caprice of a woman without enough to do? A woman who has read a lot of novels and who used to be addicted to the theatre and all that sort of thing? Do you think I am trying to make myself interesting? That I have manufactured a grand and burning passion, merely in order to amuse you? Is that what you think of me?'

The girl considered for a moment. 'No,' she said. 'I used to think that way. You were brought up in a convent, after all, and you'd never read a single novel until you married. But then I realised that a person doesn't just wreck their life in the way you have wrecked yours for the sake of mere literary effect. I know you're sincere. You couldn't help yourself.'

Something seemed to occur to the other woman.

'Tessa, let me ask you a question. Imagine a situation—tonight, for example—a situation when you suddenly felt an overwhelming urge—an imperative need, as if your life depended on it, as if it would be the culmination of your destiny—to go to some man's house right now, at once, and to stay there until morning. Would you do it?'

'Yes, I think so. If the urge was strong enough. But before giving in to it I would make a supreme effort to think of something else. And if that was no use then yes, I'd go. Tonight, straight away, in order not to change my mind and have the whole agonising process start all over again tomorrow. Because that's the real killer, I'm sure of it. I can hardly bear to look at you, in the state you're in. You can't help it, I suppose.'

'But what should I have done?' insisted the other woman.

'Something needed to happen. You remember what it was like, don't you? For a whole year you'd both been stoking your hopeless passion by gazing at each other through your opera glasses. That was the only place you saw each other, at the theatre, and then whenever there was the chance for a stolen meeting, you'd both run off in the opposite direction. And then I ended up being the poor man's go-between, bringing you all his outpourings. Perhaps it was a mistake, but I wanted to bring things to a head. So much had been said, all to no end, and the weeks and months were racing by.'

'You made me so happy then, Tessa. Just for one night. I'll never forget it. But the next day, I felt the burden on me twice as heavily. Knowing that he loved me too, but that he expected everything to come from me, that I had only so much as to lift a finger. But why should it have been me? All the responsibility, all the blame, all the guilt was to be mine. Why didn't *he* make the move?'

'Why? Because his spirit is as weak and feeble as yours is. Weak, but lacking the submissiveness of the genuinely meek. All either of you could do was rail against fate and put yourselves through days of torture, after which the only conclusion you came to was that maybe tomorrow things would change. I'm right, aren't I? Admit it.'

'Yes,' said the other woman despondently.

'I sometimes regret it now, agreeing to play the part of go-between. I misunderstood you and I think perhaps all I did was make matters worse. If I had let well alone, he would still be dreaming about you and you would still be fantasising about him and I would be sitting here listening to you pouring out your woes and you would feel better by the end of it and everything would be just as it was two years ago. It would be better that way.'

'Oh, no! I needed to know. It could have turned out to be the turning point for us. But there were so many obstacles …'

'What obstacles? I mean, yes, if it had been something the world would have considered improper, then perhaps. But he wanted you to get a divorce and become his wife.'

In reply, the other woman just laughed bitterly. 'He wanted it, you say? Then why didn't he come and carry me off, abduct me? Why didn't he summon me to his side?'

'Because you didn't give him the slightest encouragement. Quite the reverse, in fact. You looked cold and indifferent and wouldn't even give him the time of day.'

Oh, because I felt so exposed! If only you knew what was going through my head! I know about his parents—I mean, what would they have thought of me? And to bring two children into such a cold, hostile family—how could I? And—oh, I know you would have put me up, given me a roof over my head, but—well, finding a lawyer to draw up the divorce papers, that would have cost money. And I have no one. If I had a mother, or relatives of any kind—but to have to stand there and put up with all the ugly things that would be said about me, completely alone…! And while the divorce proceedings were underway—six months, perhaps—what would I have done when I needed something new to wear? I mean, who could I ask? Oh, it doesn't bear thinking about!'

The look they turned on each other then was one of sudden panic. It was as if something had snapped, some delicate gossamer thread on which their thoughts until now had hung suspended, above the grossness of the day-to-day. For some time, neither of them spoke as Tessa began examining her thoughts in a new light. Her voice was hard and deliberate when at last she said,

'You're right, Hedwig. There is no use in our talking about this. It's too late. The only thing I can wish is that he had died a couple of years ago and that you had got over it, so that it would be possible to talk to you about other things. About your husband, for example.'

'Are you out of your mind? How can you say such a thing? Or are you trying to hurt me?'

'I must say it,' came the reply, as Tessa once again touched the woman's hand. 'That man, that unfortunate cousin of mine, is too far gone. But you can go back to your husband. At first I thought it was hopeless, that you had made an utter mess of your life. But the lucky thing is that you can go back to your husband with your head held high and your honour intact. And your husband knows that.'

'No!' the other woman cried. 'I forbid you so much as to mention him. I thought I was indifferent to him but now I realise that my feelings have sickened into a kind of intense, nervous revulsion. It's not just that I don't love him; it's that he revolts me, he makes me shudder. I despise him for spinelessly putting up with everything, for just sitting it out, waiting to see if "perhaps". Well you can tell him the answer is no, never!'

'The only paths open to you are the ones that take you back to him,' Tessa urged.

'No! Look what he did to me! He ruined me!'

'He fell in love with you. He married you. That's what he did to you.'

'He desired me, he wanted to possess me, he acquired me. *That's* what he did to me. He knew I had nothing, that I was only nineteen. I went through my entire girlhood without ever once experiencing love. Which meant I wasn't even able to make a conscious choice—there *was* no choice. Of all the possible contenders, he was the only one who was prepared to feed me and keep me clothed for the rest of my life. It was as simple as that.'

'Well, but even so, you will have to go back to him. If not straight away, then sooner or later.'

'But don't you see? I can't possibly! From now on, I am nobody's, in the strictest possible sense of the word. I don't expect you to understand, but my whole soul belongs to *him*. It has done for years, ever since I first clapped eyes on him. The only time I stop thinking about him is when I really can't. I inhabit my husband's house and I look after him insofar as it is my duty to do so. But he can't expect more than that.'

A small frown appeared on Tessa's brow.

'You said something just a minute ago, Hedwig. About needing things to wear. I know it isn't tactful to say this, but look at all those nosegays of violets, in my shop. Do you think I give them away for nothing? And you, look at how well dressed you are. Your shoes are spotless, your hat is a millinery marvel. And how many pairs of gloves do you get through in a year? And dressed in all your finery, you caught that poor wretch's eye. But it was your husband who paid for it all.'

'Oh, please, Tessa, do you think that's fair? Do you think I can help the way things are, the fact that I am completely dependent on my husband's money? Did anyone ever teach me to be my own mistress? When I got married, do you think I was as wise as you are now, at the age of twenty-four? It's not that I don't work from dawn till dusk, you know. It's dull, unchallenging, soul-destroying work but I'm not too proud to do it. My word, though! Imagine if I left him and he had to engage a housekeeper. It would cost him far more and he still wouldn't be able to look after his children as well as I do.'

'His children?'

'Well, yes, all right, I know they are my children too. Goodness, don't I know it! I mean, if it weren't for them—you must believe me, Tessa, it is only the children who hold me back. Don't go thinking I care about anything else. Yes, one has to have things to wear, and if I dress stylishly, well, I think it's a matter of instinct. I do it without thinking, like walking or breathing. No, I certainly don't need his money. It doesn't cost so very much to keep body and soul together.'

'The children,' the girl insisted, imperturbably.

'Yes, the children. That is his worst crime of all. Do you think I wanted to be manacled to him by that kind of bond? I had only just been let of the convent, you know that perfectly well. I didn't give all that much thought to such things but I definitely knew that I didn't want to be a mother. I wasn't even given the chance to come round to the idea, it was just forced on me, willy-nilly. I realise that what I'm saying might sound unnatural but it's the way I feel. I could have borne all the ghastliness that goes with motherhood without batting an eyelid if life had just given me the chance to choose it of my own free will.'

'Yes, I'm sure that's true. But why are you talking this way? You're a good mother, Hedwig.'

'Yes, it's strange. It was like a miracle. In the blink of an eye, from the moment my daughter was born, I somehow became a different person. And you know I adore both of them now.'

'Yes. I never quite understood that. Your having a second child.'

'Well, how could you? But at the time my husband was still managing to convince me that I was his chattel and that his will was like some kind of unassailable law of nature. You have no idea how hard I looked for his features in my infant son's face. The features of another man, I mean, a man who could not so much as take my hand. It was like some sort of fanatical superstition. I searched and searched my son's little face, thinking about him all the time, trying to see his likeness. And now I feel as if I am more than just a mother to my children. After all, I have sacrificed everything for them—

including him. I'm not talking about my happiness, that doesn't count. It's his life I'm talking about. He's going to die.'

'Well, but what if it's hereditary? Sooner or later it was always going to happen.'

'But before it did he could have been happy for a while. You know perfectly well what torture it has been for him over the years, just as it has for me. Every divine and earthly power seemed to throw us together and yet he kept his distance. What a psychological feat of endurance that must have been! Is it any wonder he cracked under the strain?'

Once again they were silent for a while. Beyond them, in the shop, the elderly saleslady was cheerfully spraying the winter blooms, misting their frantic colours with water vapour, and the sound of her nozzle and the slight hiss of the tiny droplets repeatedly broke the silence.

Tessa was the first to speak.

'It would be better, as I've said—or at any rate, it would be for the best now—if he were to die. If he really is beyond saving, I mean. Why should he linger on for what could be years? It would be much better if he died. And time would pass, perhaps quite a lot of time, but eventually you would start to come out of it. Everything gets better with time. And as a natural part of the process, you would grow closer to your children's father. It would be some sort of solution at any rate.'

'Absolutely not! I'd rather die.'

'You won't, though. You're still healthy. You've still got thirty or maybe even forty years left in you. How paltry compared to that this two and a half years is, this two and a half years in which you have turned your whole life upside down. Even if you have been managing to cope with the misery of it. Because the time will come when you will have other things to think about. Your son's future, your daughter's wedding, your husband's final illness, and eventually your own. What you're going through now will make you smile in comparison.'

Tessa scarcely noticed that the other woman had begun to weep. She cried silently at first, with little jerking sobs that gradually turned into long-drawn-out howls of woe from deep within. Tessa left her to it. With a small, resigned sigh she stood up, paced up and down the small space a couple of times. Then she came to a halt in front of her friend.

'All right, let's try something. Even if it's too late, you might feel better if you thought we had tried to do something. I'll go and see him in the sanatorium. I'll take Grandma with me. They know her there, they know we are closely related, they'll let us in. I know that most of the time he's lucid, except for the odd intervals. I'll talk to him. I'll tell him that everything will turn out the way he wants, if only he'll just get better. You'll divorce your husband, you'll marry him. But he's got to pull himself together. Doctors often get things wrong and who knows? A severe psychological shock might be just the thing that ends up curing him. It can't hurt, can it? I'll go.'

But Hedwig now stood before her as if turned to stone. She had turned up her collar and hood and the dark fur framed her pale, interesting face, casting dark, dramatic shadows across her wide eyes and her pale, well-formed chin. It seemed to take her a while to absorb what she had just heard, to make sense of it, but then suddenly she shuddered and nervously reached towards the door handle, as if trying to stop the other woman from leaving the room.

'Don't go and see him, Tessa. Please don't, I don't want you to. I mean, why now—so suddenly? It's impossible, what good would it do? I mean, he is dying, isn't he? Nothing can save him. And in any case, the plan wouldn't work. Because after all, even if he were cured, it couldn't possibly mean I would be happy. I would just get more and more desperate, on account of the children. And—well, think of all the gossip! And his family! No, I would rather go on suffering. Because after all, it can't last much longer. Please don't go to him now. I'm too afraid of what might happen. What if it was too much of a shock for him and made his condition even worse? No, it wouldn't work.'

With trembling, feverish fingers, she fastened her satin-lined fur stole around her shoulders. Her tear-stained eyes were dry now but her mouth still quivered as she said goodbye. She turned in the doorway and bowed slightly and then said softly, in a dazed, distant, propitiatory sort of voice, as if she were talking to herself or to someone who was not fully there,

'At least—let me sleep on it. Perhaps you're right, Tessa. Perhaps it would be best to do as you suggest. But—well, we'll think about it tomorrow.'

Egy asszony meg egy leány. 1906

Endre Ady

JULIETTE GOES TO FLORENCE

Juliette pined for the embraces of her aged parents. During the course of five long, boisterous years, she had never been troubled by such pinings before. A slovenly-looking, undernourished girl, she had come up to Budapest full of a lust for life. And at such a time, a girl has other things on her mind. The first things she has to sort out are her teeth. A girl needs healthy, sharp little teeth. They need to be very dainty and pearly white. How else is she going to be able to help herself to bite-sized pieces of young men and their wallets?

Juliette had taken some good-sized bites out of life. In fact, the Budapest-engendered Juliette had completely buried Jill, the daughter of the lame old farm bailiff and his wife. And until today, she had never wanted to be reminded of the rural cottage she had run away from. But now that she could permit herself a daily scented bath, she found the village Jill coming oftener to the fore. The little cottage began to swim before her eyes, together with the little old couple, her father and mother, who must have wept salt tears over her five years ago. Tender feelings are apt to break out in girls of this type, once their skin has lost its chillblains. And Juliette had done very well for herself. Quite as befitted a farm bailiff's daughter. She had a tidy sum of money and she could afford to indulge in a few fond remembrances.

Juliette had just ended relations with her latest young beau. The poor fellow had committed a terrible crime. He had just broken into his last thousand.

On a snowy December day, Juliette wrote a letter to her father. He and her mother might have wept over her, she said, they might have grieved at her disappearance. But she was alive! She had felt impelled to leave home because she wanted to work. And she didn't want to grow old on the farmstead. But Budapest is not an unkind city. For those who don't mind working, it provides an agreeable life. She had had a lot to contend with over the past five years but now, praises be, she had a good situation. She could go back to see her beloved parents with her head held high. The holy feast of Christmas was approaching and she wanted to spend Christmas Day at home. She wanted to lay her head in her dear mother's lap, just like in the old days. She wanted to hear the farm children when they came carol singing. She wanted to play cards with her old Papa. Their own little Jill wanted to come home for a rest. Their own little Jill (that was how she signed herself).

She didn't sleep for days after posting the letter. She found herself besieged by childhood memories. She longed tearfully—desperately—to go back home. She wanted to cleanse herself, at home on the farm. So home she would go, whether they liked it or not.

When her father's answering letter arrived, she wept and laughed by turns. His clumsy, old man's handwriting seemed to shout aloud with love and joy. The old farm bailiff's ill-formed words danced with rural good humour. Come back, come home little Jill! What a blessed Christmas it will be this year! A Christmas that restores to us our long-lost child!

Cheerfully, Juliette made ready to go home. She looked out across the tall, snowy rooftops of Budapest, and in her mind's eye she saw the little cottage, imagined her father coming to fetch her from the station, imagined them jingling home together in the sleigh, while back at the farm her dear old mother was making her bedroom look festive and welcoming.

Juliette boarded her train in a fever of excitement. She began to calculate. She needed to stay on the Express until midday. Then she would have to wait at the station—oh, how hard that wait would be!—and then take the stopping train, which would get her to the station nearest home at five o'clock. From there, it was about an hour's sleigh ride. How good—how splendid! Juliette felt alternately hot and cold with anticipation.

She went into the dining car for some breakfast and found herself sitting opposite a gentleman. She did not pay him very much attention. She did not want to pay him *any* attention. Who could possibly interest her on a day like this? No one, nobody at all, except her dear, darling, beloved old parents. And one other person, her old self, Jill, the farm bailiff's daughter. Because she wasn't Juliette today. She was Jill.

But then something made her look up at her dining companion. And suddenly, she froze. She felt a sense of terrible, looming danger. She dabbed her temples with her lace handkerchief. She realised that she had broken out in a cold sweat. She mopped her brow and touched her handkerchief to her lips. And all at once, her mood changed.

It was as if Jill had suddenly tumbled off the train.

Juliette burst into a fit of the giggles.

'What have you done with your moustache, Rudolf?'

The gentleman chuckled. He had been expecting Juliette to accost him with a fit of the giggles. He simpered in return.

'It's because I'm in mourning,' he said. 'For you.'

'And where are you going, Rudolf?"

'I've no idea,' he said with a sigh. 'I'm just heading south somewhere. You know how it is with me—or you might remember.'

'Are you escaping the winter?'

'That's exactly it, Juliette my dear. The winter does terrible things to people with delicate complexions like ours. It's no good trying to keep warm. In any case, nothing can keep me warm now. Not since… Well, not since when, do you think?'

Juliette giggled again. Her heart, on the other hand was thudding. What did this mean? Why had she bumped into Rudolf, of all people? The man she thought she might even still love just a little. He had been the first man to detect the beautiful, fluttering, perfumed Juliette that lay beneath the surface of slovenly Jill the farm bailiff's daughter. And naturally, because of that, he was the man she had had to treat the most cruelly. And she had been very cruel indeed. And now she had bumped into him again. But why today of all days?

Juliette felt the need to dissemble a little. She mustn't tell him where she was going. The gentleman didn't ask. He just surveyed her features with tired, sardonic eyes. But then, in a clipped monotone, a little like a priest muttering a Hail Mary, he said,

'It's Christmas Day tomorrow. And it has occurred to Jill, the farm bailiff's daughter, that she was not born to be a Juliette. In fact, her five years in Budapest have been enough. She wants to wash Juliette out of her system, to become good, clean, wholesome Jill again. So she's going home to Mamma and Papa, to celebrate the holy feast of Christmas. But that's stuff and nonsense, Juliette. Forgive me for saying so, but it's stuff and nonsense. After five days at home you will hate the farm a good deal more than you did five years ago. And then you'll run away to Budapest again. But by that time, you will be a very embittered young woman. Embittered and with nothing left to cling to. So don't go back there, Juliette. Keep the memory of the farmstead safe. It's something you need to guard under lock and key, like a kind of talisman. Just as I preserve the memory of a pale-skinned girl, the girl I once believed could make me happy. I haven't seen her since she married. I don't want to see her. It would destroy everything. But we all need our farmstead or our pale-skinned girl, some distant token to keep locked away in our hearts. Don't go back home, little Juliette.'

By this time, Juliette had begun to cry. Through her tears she asked,

'Where should I go, then?'

'Come with me, Juliette. We'll go to Florence together. And if you don't like it, we'll go somewhere else, somewhere you *do* like. I've got a place I want to return to too, you know. And the reason I'm running away is because I want to keep that place in suspension, as a place I can tell myself will always be waiting for me.'

JULIETTE GOES TO FLORENCE

The express train pulled in to the station where Juliette was supposed to get off. She stood up, collected her belongings, prepared to alight. Then she looked at the young man's face. She collapsed in a heap of tears. She buried her face in her shawl. Rudolf jumped onto the platform. The train still had a few minutes to wait. When he got back on he said,

'It's all arranged, little Juliette. You're coming with me. To Florence.'

The train set off. With a strangled cry, Juliette ran to the window. Snaking off into the distance, she saw the branch line, along which the stopping train would go. A wide, white world lay beyond it. She seemed to hear a jingling of bells. The old farm bailiff would be setting off for the station on his sleigh. Setting off to collect his daughter Jill, who was on her way home for the holy feast of Christmas.

Juliette Firenzébe megy. 1907

Zsigmond Móricz

SEVEN FARTHINGS

The gods performed an act of mercy when they endowed the poor with the gift of laughter. It is not only a wailing and a gnashing of teeth that one hears emanating from their hovels; there is plenty of hearty merriment, too. In fact, it is often the case that a poor person will laugh in circumstances that would reduce any normal individual to tears.

I am pretty well acquainted with the world. The generation of the Soós family to which my father belonged plumbed the very depths of indigence. That was when my father worked as a hired hand in the machine factory. He never boasted about how things were in those days. No one else did either. It was just a fact.

What is also a fact is that never again in my life have I laughed as hard as I did during those years of my early childhood.

How could I have done, after all, with no rosy-cheeked, merry mother to laugh with me? My mother had such a way with laughter. She would laugh so hard that her eyes filled with tears. And then a fit of coughing would come over her and she would cough so hard that she almost choked.

But even my mother never laughed harder than on that day we spent searching for seven farthings. We sought—and we found. Three in the drawer of her sewing machine table and one in the china cupboard. The other three were harder to unearth.

It was my mother who found the first three. She worked as a seamstress and when people paid her, she always put the money in her sewing machine drawer. In fact, she had expected to find rather more than just three farthings there. But that drawer was my Ali Baba's cave. All I had to do was put my hand on the knob and say 'Open, sesame…!' It was a treasure trove.

So while my mother rummaged around in it, I just stood and stared. She rummaged for a long time, turning out pins, thimbles, scissors, lengths of ribbon, buttons. Eventually, dumbfounded, she said,

'They're hiding.'

'What are?'

'The farthings—little beggars!' She burst into laughter. She pulled the drawer out completely. 'Come on, boy. We can't let them give us the slip. We've got to find those naughty, naughty farthings.'

She squatted down on the floor, bringing the drawer with her, holding it very carefully, as if she was afraid that the farthings might somehow fly away. Then, with a sudden swift movement, she tipped it over, like when someone swipes their hat over a butterfly to ensnare it.

It was impossible not to laugh.

'They're in there all right, they can't escape,' she chortled. 'Even if there is only a single farthing in there, it can't get away.

I crouched down on the floor beside her, watching the drawer carefully in case any shiny coins tried to make a dash for it. Nothing moved. The fact was, we had begun to doubt that we were going to find anything. We looked at each other and burst out laughing. I reached out and touched the upside-down drawer.

'Careful, now!' my mother said. 'We don't want them to get away. You're still too young to know what a sly creature a farthing is. It has a knack of disappearing as quick as a flash. Oh my, how it can roll!'

We each looked about us, contorting ourselves to look into every cranny. We both had plenty of experience of how farthings excelled at rolling.

When we had searched everywhere, I reached out my hand again, as if to turn over the drawer.

'Oi!' said Mother, sternly, and I snatched my hand back, as if I had just burned it on the red-hot stove.

'Watch what you're doing, you little scamp! Don't be in such a hurry to let that farthing get away. While it's trapped under that drawer, it's ours. Let's just let it cool its heels for a bit. It's my wash day, you see, which means I need soap, and for a cake of soap I need at least seven farthings. They won't give it to me for less than seven. Well, I've got three and I need four more and they're hiding under here but they don't like being disturbed and if they think they're being badgered, they have a habit of making themselves scarce. So we've got to be careful. Money is sensitive, you see, one has to treat it very gingerly. With respect. One has to approach it delicately, in the way one would approach a fine lady. You don't know any pretty verses, by any chance? Something one could use to coax it to come out?'

How we laughed at our own silliness! But I came up with a ditty all the same:

'Ladybird, farthing-bird, fly to our home,

Your house is on fire and your children are gone…'

And with that I turned over the drawer.

A great heap of stuff lay underneath it, but not a single farthing could we find amongst the muddle. My mother sifted through it again and again, her lips drawn into a grim line.

'What a pity we don't have a table,' she said. 'If we had a table, we could have tipped the drawer out on that. That would have been more respectful, you see, and the money might have shown itself.'

I gathered up all the bits and pieces and bundled them back in the drawer. Meanwhile, my mother racked her brains, trying to think of somewhere she might have tucked away a coin or two, but she drew a blank. But then I had a sudden idea.

'I know, Mother! I know a place where there'll be a farthing!'

'Where, my boy? Quick, let's find it before it melts away like snow.'

'In the drawer of the china cupboard.'

'Gracious, how fortunate that you didn't say so before! Otherwise it would have vanished by now.'

We got to our feet and went over to the china cupboard—which had not had any china in it for many a year. But in its drawer, we found a farthing. As I had known we would. I had been planning to filch it for three days but had not plucked up the courage. If my courage hadn't failed me, I would have used it to buy sweets.

'Well, that brings it up to four farthings. Never despair, my boy! We've got more than half what we need. All we need now is three more. Let me see—it's taken us an hour to find the first four. That means we will have all seven by teatime. That still gives me time to do the laundry before nightfall. Come on, let's search all the drawers in case there's a farthing in each of them.'

If that had been the case, we would have had a merry surplus. Because in its youth, that old china cupboard had been destined for a household with fripperies a-plenty. Alas, we scarcely put it to any use at all, poor battered, worm-eaten old thing.

Before opening each drawer, my mother uttered a kind of little incantation.

'This drawer was once a rich drawer. This one never had a bean. This one lived its entire life on tick. And this one— miserable old vagrant—is it possible that its pockets will turn out to be empty, too? And this one certainly won't yield anything. This is where our own pennilessness is kept. And this one? No, I'm not expecting anything in here. I've already asked it once and it didn't want to oblige me. But *this* one,' she cried, tugging open the last drawer (a drawer which no longer even had a bottom), 'this one is filled with gold!'

She flung her arms round my neck and we fell to the floor laughing.

'Wait!' she said suddenly, 'I've got it! There'll be money in your father's pockets!'

My father's clothes hung on a row of nails banged into the wall. And sure enough, in the first pocket my mother tried, she found a farthing.

She could hardly believe her eyes.

'I've found one!' she cried. 'Look! How many is that now? So many I've lost count. One—two—three—four—five! Five! We only need two more. And what are two farthings? Nothing. Where there are five, there must be another two.'

Eagerly, she set about checking all my father's other pockets, but sadly she had no luck. She didn't find a single farthing more. Nothing she could think of would conjure up those missing two. Two burning red spots appeared on her cheeks. That is what happened to my mother when she got over-excited or worked too hard. She wasn't really supposed to work at all, it always made her ill. Though of course, what we were doing wasn't really work. The pursuit of money is something that everyone is allowed to indulge in.

Teatime came and went. Dusk began to fall. My father needed a clean shirt for the next day and there was no way of laundering one for him. Well-water on its own wasn't enough to get the grease out.

But then my mother clapped a hand to her forehead.

'Oh! Oh, what an ass I am! I haven't even checked my own pockets! But now that I've thought of it, let's have a look.'

And she did. And hey presto! She found a farthing. Number six.

'Now let's have a look in your pockets,' she said. 'In case there's a farthing there, too.'

My pockets! Well, I turned them out. But there were no farthings lurking in them.

It was almost dark and there we were with six farthings. Six, which for our purposes were no better than one. The shopkeeper never let people have things on credit and our neighbours were all as poor as we were. There was no point trying to borrow a farthing from any of them.

There was nothing we could do but laugh at our misfortune.

And then a beggar came to our door. In a thin and wheedling voice, he launched into his patter. My mother looked dazed at first but soon began to laugh in his face.

'You can save your breath, my good fellow,' she told him. 'Here I've been all afternoon, twiddling my thumbs because I lack the money for a half-pound cake of soap. I've got one farthing too few.'

The beggar, a kindly-faced old man, just stared at her and said, 'One farthing?'

'That's right.'

'I'll give it to you.'

'What? Alms from a beggarman? Whatever next!'

'Don't be afraid to take it, my good woman. After all, I don't need it. All I need now is a shovelful of earth to cover my bones. That'll see me right.'

He pressed the farthing into my hand and tottered away, muttering his thanks.

'Well, praises be!' said my mother. 'Run along now, my boy…'

But then she stopped. She burst out laughing. She laughed

so hard she couldn't stop.

'A fine time to have got the money together at last! It's too late, it's pitch dark. I can't do any laundry now. I'll need money for the lamp. We're out of oil!'

And suddenly she was laughing so hard she began to choke. She was racked with great heaving, rasping spasms, so violent that I had to run to her and hold her up. And as she leaned against me, with her hands pressed flat against her cheeks, I felt something warm trickling onto my arm.

It was blood. My mother's life blood. The precious, hallowed blood of my own dear mother, a woman who knew how to laugh so heartily, so well. She laughed like no one else I have ever known.

Hét krajcár. 1908

Károly Lovik

THE SILENT CRIME

I

In a small provincial coffee house, five army officers were making an evening of it. Two of them were playing billiards and two others, half-sprawled across the mottled marble tabletop, were jeering at their comrades' botched shots. The fifth, a heavily built Regimental Medical Officer, with a beard that skimmed the outline of his jaw, was sitting in a corner studying the bill of fare. It was a typical dull, small-town evening in high summer. The sounds of an accordion and the clinking of tankards drifted in from the next-door beer garden. Loud curses and vulgar backchat emanated from the baker's shop on the left. The small front room of the coffee house was lit by a dripping oil lamp that cast only a wan light on the billiard table. On the ceiling it cast a little more illumination, revealing the fat flies that crawled about on the pockmarked plaster. The billiard game, contested between a long-legged Lieutenant in buckskin breeches and a baby-faced, rosy-cheeked Second Lieutenant, was beginning to be dull. One of the idle onlookers gave a yawn; the other began playing with the coins in his pocket. They had been stationed in this town for two weeks now, and were longing to move on.

At that moment, the door opened and in came a small man dressed in plain-weave. The long-legged Lieutenant gave a suppressed smirk and put down his billiard cue. The baby-faced Second Lieutenant, attempting to hide a similar smirk, slunk over to the girl behind the till. The other officers regarded the newcomer with amused condescension.

The man in plain-weave was employed in some kind of clerical capacity at the local land registry or tax office. But the soldiers did not inquire too nearly into his social or financial circumstances. It was enough for them that they could have some sport with him. And Mr Burián gave them ample opportunity. He always took the soldiers' japes in good part; indeed, he felt flattered that they took so much notice of him. Every evening he would come to the coffee house, drink a glass of milk and read the newspapers. Then he would take out his horn-rimmed eyeglass—which, with his sunken, clean-shaven face, made him look for all the world like an old crone doing the darning—surreptitiously draw his chair a little closer to the officers and settle down to listen to their raillery. He never sought to involve himself in their conversation of his own accord. He sat hunched in his chair as if everlastingly begging their pardon, and fixed his slow gaze on the legs of the billiard table. If any of the soldiers addressed him, he became flustered, began stroking his chin and stammering a response, his eyes round with alarm.

The little clerk would stay in the coffee house until half past eight, at which time he would pick up his battered green umbrella, take his leave of the company with an obsequious bow, and set off home.

The officers all teased him mercilessly. Once, they filled his coat pockets with heavy stones. Another time, they hid a mouse in his umbrella. Then they stuffed paper under the rim of his hat and persuaded him that all the milk he drank was making his head swell. They made him believe that a goods train had come off the rails at the station and had crashed its way through town. They put effervescent tablets in his water glass, and laughed as the contents shot skywards when he filled it. For want of any other diversion, this suited the officers very well and it cost them nothing. And Mr Burián did not seem to mind their ribbing. Each day he would come to the coffee house as usual, and with a shy smile would remark,

'The young gentlemen were in high spirits again last night.'

Anyone would think he was proud to be made sport of.

On this particular evening, when Mr Burián came in, one of the officers called out,

'No milk for you tonight, my friend! It's my name day. You shall be my guest.'

Mr Burián's eyes flicked nervously to and fro. He began to gesticulate and then finally brought out,

'Oh sir, I'm sure you do me a great honour… Far beyond my deserts… But I never take wine.'

The Lieutenant dismissed his words with a wave of the hand. 'For shame, my man! It's time that error was corrected. This is on me!'

The waiter brought a bottle of wine and six glasses. The officers drank a toast and Mr Burián was forced to drink some wine as well. And as he did so, he became aware of something very curious. The wine rasped his throat at first and seemed to sear his chest, but then all of a sudden it began to feel rather agreeable, filling his stomach with a warm glow. The second glass slipped down much more easily. But when the men put a third glass in front of him, he suddenly remembered his home and his long face grew grave. Before his eyes swam a vision of his wife, staring intently at her embroidery frame, and his son, tucked up in bed, little suspecting what bad habits his father was getting into. He stood up, and humbly bowing his head, said,

'Thank you, Sir. I feel I have drunk enough today. Gentlemen…'

'Surely you aren't leaving?' exclaimed one of the officers with pugnacious bonhomie. We haven't had a song yet, dear Country Cousin.'

'If you please not to take it the wrong way, Sir, but I must go… My boy is not quite himself…'

'That's no excuse at all, Burián! Surely you wouldn't wish to offend us all?'

The little clerk blushed to the roots of his hair. The very idea that he should be the cause of a rift between the army and the citizens of the town, even perhaps leading to a duel!

'Heaven forfend!' he stammered, and drank another glass of wine.

But it proved to be too much of a good thing. He felt as if the coffee house had slowly started to spin, taking him along with it, as if on a fairground carousel. Everything seemed so merry: the pictures on the walls, the mirror, the waiters, the girl behind the till, the soldiers' pet dogs. The billiard table seemed to be dancing a two-step. Mr Burián closed his eyes but the feeling didn't go away. In fact, he saw exactly the same things but this time they had fiery circles round them. A pleasant drowsiness set in. If he had not been sitting with the officers, he would have fallen fast asleep.

The Lieutenant signalled to the baby-faced Second Lieutenant, who plucked a long, paper waitress's headband[21], colourfully ruffled, from the cash desk and surreptitiously tucked it into Burián's collar. As he sat there with his head hanging forward and with the blue and red tapes of the paper headband pointing upwards, he looked for all the world like a puppet on a string. That was tonight's little joke. The silly fellow was bound not to notice his extra accessory and would happily set off across town with it.

And indeed, Mr Burián was perfectly unsuspecting. In his semi-slumber he had a vision of his wife, diligently stitching at her embroidery. He stood to his feet.

'I really must go,' he said bashfully, taking up his umbrella. 'My deep respects, gentlemen.'

The soldiers permitted him to depart. They drank the remainder of the wine, then took themselves through to the dining-room.

2

Mr Burián slowly wended his way home. Every so often he stopped, listening to the distant strains of music, then plucked some jasmine fronds from a bush, deciding he would take them home to his wife. He was aware of a strange tickling feeling around his neck and flapped at it with his hand.

'Why won't it go?' he muttered. 'Pesky fly!'

But the fly wouldn't go.

'Well, if that's the way you like it,' Mr Burián chuckled, 'then come along. You'll clear off soon enough when you've been on starvation rations for a couple of days, because you'll find my cupboard sadly bare.'

And so saying, he gave no more thought to the fly, and the long tapes from the paper headband trailed behind him as he went. Passers-by turned to look and tittered, but Mr Burián was completely oblivious. He picked his way, with his eyes fixed on the road, because he had the odd feeling that the cobbles were trying to slither from under his feet.

He got home to find his wife in the kitchen, breaking ice with a hand axe. Breaking ice? Mr Burián looked perplexedly at the gaunt, careworn woman, who was standing with her back to him and didn't notice him come in. But in an instant his perplexity gave way to a lurching dread. It crossed his mind that when the Municipal Chief Constable had been on his deathbed, they had broken ice in the kitchen, too.

'Is anyone ill?' he asked tremulously.

His wife turned, put down the axe and suddenly burst into a storm of tears.

'Who is it?' her husband asked again, beads of sweat breaking out on his brow.

His wife pointed towards the inner room. Mr Burián threw down his umbrella and rushed to the doorway, his eyes wide with fright.

In the poky, poorly-lit room stood the local physician, taking the child's pulse. The little boy was lying quite still, half on one side, his eyes staring at the ceiling. But it was clear from his breathing that he was unwell. He seemed to be struggling for air; his throat rattled and his lungs wheezed.

Mr Burián ran to the sick boy's bedside and seized his hand. It seemed to be on fire.

'What's wrong, my own sweet son, what's wrong?' he gasped, the tears streaming down his pale cheeks.

The child made no reply but continued staring silently at the ceiling.

'Doctor!' cried Mr Burián, falling to his knees at the physician's feet. 'What has happened to my poor little boy? What is to be done?' His whole body shook as he spoke. 'Dear Lord, I implore you, take *my* life instead! I beg you, take *my* life instead…'

The physician washed his hands.

'It is very serious, I'm afraid,' he said in a low voice. 'I should like to get a second opinion.'

'The Regimental Medical Officer?' whispered Mr Burián. 'Might we ask him?'

The physician nodded. 'Yes. I shall fetch him now, and on my way I will look in at the druggist's.' He took up his hat. 'Put a fresh poultice on the child's neck while I am gone.'

Mr Burián was left alone with the boy. He sat down beside him on the bed, leaning over him so that their heads were touching, and stroked his sweaty, matted hair with a trembling hand.

'Dear boy, would you like to play with some of your toys?' he mumbled softly, his eyes scanning the ragged puppets and three-legged wooden animals in the child's room.

The boy did not reply. He seemed to have aged immeasurably. He stood staring straight ahead, as if pondering the answer to some deep question.

'Dear child, say something!' his father pleaded. 'Talk to your Papa. Have I not always loved you more than anyone else in the world? My dearest own one, just one little word!'

The boy stirred, and now his eyes were fixed on a point somewhere above his father's head.

'The funeral has begun,' he said. 'The horse has arrived.'

Mr Burián looked at his boy in horror. He could not bring himself to answer. He began to weep, with thin, whimpering sobs, like a helpless wretch.

The boy kept staring above his father's head.

'There's the horse,' he went on, a deathly croak accompanying each word. 'I can see its plumes tossing.'

Mr Burián turned a trembling head to look behind him. But all he saw was a blank wall. 'There's nothing there, little one,' he faltered. 'Don't be frightened.'

'But it's got a plume!' the boy persisted weakly. 'I can see it clearly, Father.'

His little face was pinched. He turned his solemn eyes to the ceiling once more. Mr Burián stood up. Holding his head in his hands, he stood and waited, for something—anything. Perhaps he was waiting for the miracle that would banish this ghastly nightmare. He was appalled by his own littleness. How powerless he was, not strong enough to tackle so much as a fly, certainly not this horror which was rumbling inexorably towards him.

The door opened and the two doctors and his wife came

in. The Regimental Medical Officer looked round the room. His eyes came to rest on the bed. He lifted the child into a sitting position while Mr Burián's wife lit candles so that he could see into the boy's throat. He pursed his lips, looking hard at the little clerk. The physician understood. He took the boy's mother into the next room.

'My friend,' said the Regimental Medical Officer gravely—a tone of voice that Mr Burián had never heard him use before—'it's very serious. You are a grown man. I shall speak plainly.'

Mr Burián felt as though his knees would give way.

'This must come to us all,' the Medical Officer intoned. 'And…' His eyes, which until now had been avoiding those of the little clerk, fell squarely upon him. There, behind the distraught man's two large ears, bobbed the token of their evening's little prank. Long strips of blue and red paper fluttered to and fro, tangling themselves in the clerk's sparse hair.

From the direction of the bed came a dull, hacking cough, as if someone was beating nails into a coffin. Mr Burián ran towards the sound, as if to do battle with an invisible enemy. He did not notice the Regimental Medical Officer plucking the headband from his collar and stuffing it into his pocket.

3

The boy died in the early hours of the morning.

The Regimental Medical Officer returned to his barracks, ill-humoured and scowling. The regiment had just got back from exercises and the young Second Lieutenant sat grinning astride his frisky mount. It was a beautiful summer's day. The little town was bathed in sunshine, while a gentle easterly breeze dallied in the linden trees. The Regimental Medical Officer nodded towards the Second Lieutenant.

'D'you know what happened to that poor old fellow we were teasing last night?' he said gloomily.

The Second Lieutenant laughed. His eyes kept flitting to a little low house where the net curtains fluttered to and fro.

'Somewhat the worse the wear for drink?' he suggested idly.

The Medical Officer fixed him with a steely glare. 'His young son died at dawn,' he said quietly.

The Second Lieutenant stiffened. The little low house was instantly forgotten. Deep down, he wasn't a bad fellow. He just fell in with what he saw everyone else doing but if it came to it, he wouldn't hurt a fly. At the thought of last night's prank, the colour flew to his cheeks.

'Poor devil… I could curse myself!' he bit out.

The Medical Officer shrugged. Then he said, 'Perhaps the poor child is better off where he is. But there's one thing I can't get out of my head. Do you know what the last thing he said was? He saw a hearse coming towards him, drawn by a horse, and he said, "Please don't take me!"'

'Was he delirious?'

The Medical Officer dropped his gaze. 'Only partly. He thought that the paper streamers hanging from his father's neck were the plumes on a horse's head. A horse that was pulling a hearse.'

The Second Lieutenant turned pale and just stared at his

companion. He was filled with self-loathing. The japes of the night before seemed the lowest of all low tricks. At that very moment, he would happily have endorsed the opinion of anyone who abused him for a vile wretch and broke his sword across his back. He could exactly imagine the scene: the sick boy gasping for air, the mean little room, the father beside himself with grief while all the time, above his shrivelled little old-crone's face, the paper streamers bobbed and jigged.

He jumped from his horse, pulled his cap down hard over his eyes and blundered off into the fields. His ears were ringing, he was overcome by a kind of physical revulsion, as if some poisonous serum had been poured into his veins. Anyone who came his way stepped hastily aside and a dog who came trotting along beside an elderly peasant suddenly took off after him, barking like a hyena.

He had no idea how far he walked. From time to time he stopped, gnawing at his lip, then he mopped his brow and hurried on. Feeling that destruction might bring relief, he began slashing furiously with his riding crop at the wayside flowers. But nothing could banish the vision of the sick boy. In his mind's eye he saw him clearly, with blue lips and staring eyes, transfixed by the apparition of a hearse and its plumed horse.

When at last he pulled himself together, he decided to pay Mr Burián a visit.

He found the little clerk sitting staring into space, in front of a cheerless cottage with peeling plaster. Funeral preparations were underway in the yard. An undertaker was going in and out and the neighbours' children were standing in a silent huddle in front of the shrouded windows. A meagre little wreath, woven from evergreen branches and meadow flowers, was suspended under the deep eaves.

The Second Lieutenant came to a standstill in front of Mr Burián and doffed his cap.

'Forgive us!' he muttered, holding out his hand.

Mr Burián rose, bowed humbly and looked at the soldier in amazement. 'What is it you ask of me, Sir?' he said diffidently, likewise removing his own head covering.

The Second Lieutenant could not bear to meet his eyes.

'I'm asking you to forgive us for last night…for that tasteless joke!' he said, biting his lip.

Mr Burián did not know what to say. Nervously he stroked his chin, which seemed to have grown more wizened and shrunken overnight, and looked up with an unsteady gaze.

'Could you do that?' the Second Lieutenant asked again. Catching sight of the wreath that hung under the eaves, he hung his head.

The little clerk made an effort to recover himself. 'But I have nothing to forgive the young gentlemen for,' he stammered. 'You have always been so gracious to me… Why, the Regimental Medical Officer was here all night, and would take nothing from me for his pains. It is I who should thank *you*, for always taking such trouble over a poor devil like myself.'

The Second Lieutenant saw that it was useless and his conscience pricked him the harder for it.

Hanging his head, he asked, 'Would you let me have a flower from that wreath?'

Mr Burián stumbled dolefully to where the wreath hung and pulled out a sprig of jasmine. Wordlessly, the Second Lieutenant put it in his pouch, then shook the little clerk by the hand.

'God bless you!' he said. 'And may your son's soul rest in peace.'

'For ever and ever amen!' mumbled Mr Burián, crossing himself.

The Second Lieutenant walked slowly home along the highway. He felt as if his carefree youth had been destroyed forever by some nameless, silent crime. A crime for which he would never be required to make amends and for which no one would ever give him a bad name, but which would haunt him for the rest of his life, more painful than losing a brother.

A néma bűn. Published posthumously

Dezső Kosztolányi

THE CABARET SINGER'S MIRACULOUS COMEBACK

1

They buried Krisztina Hrussz, the cabaret singer, on the 7th of January 1902. The ceremony took place at three in the afternoon. There had been a hard frost and it was already dark by the time the coffin was taken out to the yard and hoisted onto the bier. It would receive a final blessing before being loaded into the hearse. The priest's nose was rosehip red with the cold. The taste of his luncheon still lingered in his mouth, the spicy zest of the Badacsony[22] wine he had drunk. Now angels and roses seemed to float before his eyes in the mist. He raised aloft the phial of holy water. By his side stood Vidor Tass, the young medical student, the cabaret singer's faithful swain and now the focus of all eyes. Dressed in a suit of unkempt black, he was mastering his grief with quiet dignity. Among the other mourners were a handful of seasoned dance-hall troupers, one serious artist type and the manager of the cabaret theatre. Almost all of them were thoroughly enjoying themselves. Surrounded by this atmosphere of mourning, they were mainly still thinking of the lunch they had all just eaten. A healthy measure of epicureanism served to leaven the melancholy of the occasion.

Later, when the last rites were concluded and the horses, tossing their gloomy plumes, had clopped off towards the cemetery, their route illuminated by lamps and torches, a heavy rain began to fall. It coated the coffin in a veneer of ice, so that from a distance it appeared to be made of glass. Ice soon covered everything, a glistening membrane turning all it touched to crystal and sugarplums and conjuring a skating rink from the tarmac. But it did not last. Frozen feet soon found themselves shuffling through a dolorous icy slush. The funeral cortège turned up towards the hill. Vidor watched its shadowy, flickering progress, ethereal in the early afternoon. He was struck more with awe and wonder than with grief. It was all so difficult to believe. Three days ago, Krisztina had caught pneumonia. And now she was gone, swiftly and cruelly snatched away, like someone blindfolded in the night, bundled into a carriage and spirited off to face the new dawn elsewhere. That was what Vidor found so extraordinary. He did not really believe in death. The chanting of the mourners filled his ears, the Latin lamentations—and his thoughts turned to cake and hot chocolate.

Slapping fresh mortar between the bricks, the masons finished walling up the crypt. Vidor was alone by the time he came down the hill. His arms hung limply by his sides. He thought about the dead girl and groaned. Once again, he was overcome by the painful strangeness of it all. He looked around for Krisztina and—oh! Oh woe! Of course, she was not there.

2

Later, at home, he wept. Hunched over the little table under the dim window, he wept bitterly and copiously. He did not bother to undress for the night. For three days he scarcely slept. The minutes, hours, days all melted into one. When a glimmer of light shone through the shutter slats, he did not know if it was dawn or sunset.

If only she would come back to me! he sobbed into his pillow.

With the approach of spring he grew calmer, but his face was noticeably paler than before. He was no longer able to weep outright but his tears still seemed to flow inside him. The new passivity of his grief was fearful to behold. Those who saw him were at a loss for words.

If only she would come back to me! he sighed.

In the evenings, he would spread out her clothes: her shoes; the yellow *foulard* she used to twirl so charmingly about her neck. He imagined her sitting beside him by the fire, on a chair or on the floor, with her sweet, daintily freckled face turned towards the warm red glow. He often pictured her in his bed. He heard her voice. Whenever his doorbell rang, he raced to open it and was crestfallen when it was not her. He would return to his room, feigning a reunion in meticulous detail. Krisztina would come in. He would help her off with her coat. He would offer her a seat but Krisztina would fling her arms about his neck, burying her head in his chest, laughing merrily. He fantasised in this way until dawn, listening to her laughter, gazing into her eyes. After a night of ghostly embraces, he would waken grey-faced, a bitter taste on his tongue.

Every night he went to the cabaret, scanning the tawdry little stage for her face among the lurid lights. He never found it. He stayed until midnight, then went home, but he found no comfort there. With mounting alarm he realised that, at least in his case, time was not the great healer. His lost beloved seemed more beautiful than she had ever been. Through the veil of the years her freckles seemed to shine more golden and more radiant, like lovely erogenous little dots. Her lips were like twin rubies and the silvery spittle on her tongue a warm, emollient balm.

If only she would come back to me!

His sighs became a religious longing, the distilled quintessence of his sorrow and his grief. He could not free himself of his desire; he would give his life just to see her again, if only for a moment. That single moment, in his mind, took on a metaphysical dimension. The whole sum of human bliss, he felt, would be contained within that fleeting space.

As time wore on, his longings became more modest. If I were but to see her coffin again, he said to himself; just to peep through its glass panel, to catch a glimpse of her clothing. Just a flicker, a passing shadow. Would it have been her lace that he saw—or just a scudding cloud? Oh, but to be granted a sight of it he would go for years bare-headed, on bleeding, unshod feet! In company, at dance parties, surrounded by bouncing good humour, these fantasies would engulf him with a sudden frisson. There was no escape; they pursued him. Dumbly, he succumbed to his new role as a shadowy familiar of his dead beloved. Pale and gaunt, he stalked her in the moonlight. His speech became stilted, his dress developed a chilly sheen. His shirtfront shone like a memorial tablet in some dingy vault, ghastly white and glimmering, so that all who saw him remembered the dead girl, her sleeping head now filled for eternity with unarticulated dreams.

If only she would come back to me!

The yearning rocked his heart. It was written across his features. Pain scored deep lines into the wax of his cheeks. All the years of misery and woe were hardened now, cold and set like a death mask.

3

And then, one day, Krisztina came back.

4

One sultry afternoon in May, after a riotous night, carousing on the town, Vidor Tass was on his way home.

All along the Nagykörút boulevard[23], the acacia trees were frenziedly flinging their scent into the air. Thrusting up from the pavement, bowing and branching, they trumpeted their fragrance to the sky.

Vidor felt faint from the cacophony of their perfume. Nausea gripped his stomach. Sulphurous streaks were worming their way across a distant edge of the horizon, muted flashes of colour, as if someone were playing with a mirror in a darkened room.

Onward and homeward he went.

The maid met him in the hall.

'There's someone to see you, sir.'

'Who is it?'

'A lady.'

Vidor Tass was taken aback. He could not imagine who his visitor might be. He had not received a single lady in his rooms since Krisztina's death.

He opened his door.

And there, sitting on the bed, was Krisztina. The yellow *foulard* was wound round her neck. Her face was placid, almost merry.

'Krisztina!' he breathed.

'Darling!' she replied, coming to nestle against him.

Somehow, Vidor did not feel at all surprised. He struck a match and lit two candles. By their light, he could see Krisztina plainly. Death had done her a power of good. She looked in far better health than she had done when alive. She had even put on a bit of weight. She was well turned out, neat as a new pin. Her white dress—the same dress she had been buried in—looked soft against her skin. It suited her. It was true that it was slightly frayed around the hem and that here and there—though not so that anyone would really notice—it was sprigged with mildew. At the sides it was dusted with saltpetre crystals, the sequins of the sepulchre. She held out her hand.

'See—my ring.'

'Your ring—it really is!'

A question sprang to Vidor's lips but Krisztina shook her head.

'No questions,' she protested. 'I'm here, as you can see. Fresh as a daisy. Don't imagine this is some kind of supernatural ghost story. I'm not a ghost or a spirit. But I haven't got time to explain. I can only stay for half an hour. After that, I shall have to go back. Take out your watch. It's three o'clock now. By half past three, I'll be gone.'

'Only thirty minutes!' moaned Vidor.

But Krisztina did not like this display of emotion.

'Don't be so melodramatic, darling,' she said. 'Each one of those minutes is worth its weight in gold.'

'Oh, a thousand times!' her lover cried. 'Your kiss—your kiss is worth a thousand times more!'

'Well? You've been summoning me for eight years. Now your time has come. So what are you waiting for?'

Krisztina held out her arms. Her rosy lips parted, eagerly inviting his kiss.

Vidor kissed her.

Then they sat, Vidor on a stool, Krisztina on the couch, and stared at each other. They stared at each other mutely. Was it that the kiss had been a disappointment? They each began to feel a little sheepish. Vidor dropped his gaze. Was this really the reunion he had dreamed of for so long? What kind of a meeting *was* this? He felt as if it had all happened much too fast. What was he supposed to do? The room was filled with a heavy silence. He could hear his heart beating, saw the hands of his watch creeping slowly round the dial.

Only five minutes had passed. They still had twenty-five to go. Suddenly, the time seemed impossibly long. The silence became ever more awkward.

Vidor coughed.

'How are you?' he asked. 'I mean, what news?'

Krisztina's eyes flew wide. It had clearly been tactless to ask such a question of the dead.

'Shall I make some tea?' Vidor suggested quickly.

'No, not for me, thank you.'

'You…' He stopped. 'You know that Herman got married? Three years ago now. They've got a child. A son. Strong, healthy little boy.'

'That's nice,' Krisztina said, sounding bored.

'And—well—lots of other things have happened besides that. My father died, of stomach cancer. He was in agony, poor fellow.'

'That's nice.'

'Well, not very, eh? But apart from that—I've qualified. I've got my doctor's license. I'm planning to start my own practice next year. I'm buying the flat next door. I'll have four rooms, a bathroom, kitchen, electric lighting…'

'That's nice.'

'Nessa's theatrical career has been a total flop.'

'That's nice.'

'But Illy has been a roaring success. Audiences go wild for her.'

'That's nice.'

Vidor felt his throat go tight. He stole a look at his watch and saw that Krisztina had only been with him for seven minutes. Frantically, he tried to think of something else to say. Every minute seemed an eternity. At first, he thought he should try something witty, but then it occurred to him that a more serious note was called for. In the end he decided that neither would do, and so he said nothing. Another whole minute went by without either of them uttering a syllable. Krisztina sat on the couch with her eyes on the floor, studying the patterns in the carpet.

Meanwhile, it had started to rain.

'It's raining,' said Vidor.

'Yes,' said Krisztina.

'It was lovely weather yesterday, though.'

'Yes.'

'It's blowing quite a gale out there!'

'Yes.'

Then he suddenly changed the subject.

'Aren't you cold in that thin dress?'

'No!' laughed Krisztina.

They exchanged a few more words, made a renewed effort, and then relapsed into silence again. They looked at each other blankly. Vidor stood up, as if by doing so he could extricate himself from his embarrassment. Only nine minutes had elapsed. Krisztina leaned back on the couch. Vidor stood by the window. Krisztina suddenly became aware of a tugging sensation in her jaw. She wanted to shout out loud how bored she was and then run, flee the oppression of this room. Her muscles twitched, pulled her mouth wide open. Involuntarily, like an automaton, she gave an almighty yawn. Not once, not twice, but three times. Then she picked up her umbrella and walked towards the door. For a moment, she seemed about to speak, but as her hand touched the door handle she was overcome by a further paroxysm of yawning. Without another word, she left the room.

Vidor was alone once more. And instantly, he was filled with a surge of relief, of release. His fingers drummed a short tattoo on the tabletop. He looked out at the street, at the umbrellas, at the storm, at the rainwater streaming down the window pane. He shrugged. He yawned. He looked at his watch. It was ten past three.

They could have had another twenty minutes.

Hrussz Krisztina csodálatos látogatása. 1911

Géza Csáth
LITTLE EMMA

The story that follows comes from the diary of a distant relative of mine who took his own life at the age of twenty. His mother recently died too, and her son's diaries came to me. It was some time before I got round to looking at them. I began reading them a short while ago and the open, honest style of the writing surprised me. The extraordinary account reproduced below comes from the third notebook. I have done no more than shorten it slightly and make a few corrections to the punctuation.

Little Emma was the prettiest of all my sister Irma's friends. I always loved her blonde hair, her grey eyes and her delicate little face.

I was in my second year of primary school. Emma and Irma were in the year below. All the other boys liked Emma too but they didn't talk about her. They would have been embarrassed to be seen to be bothering about a girl, especially one who was in the junior year. I, on the other hand, immediately knew that I loved her; and although I was also embarrassed about this, I made up my mind that I would always love her and that one day I would make her my wife.

Little Emma often came round to our house. We would all play together, with my two younger sisters and my elder brother Gábor. Sometimes, other girls came as well. Our cousins Anni and Juci, for example, on whom we practised kisses in the cellar or the attic, or the garden or the woodshed.

It was a beautiful, warm September. I appreciated the fine weather much more than I had the sunshine of summer because we were made to sit in the classroom all afternoon from two until four as well as in the morning from eight till eleven, and after that the fresh air and the ball games seemed so much better. We never got sick of playing. We went home for tea and then carried on messing around until it was supper time.

School seemed more interesting and enjoyable that year, too. Our new teacher, Mihály Szladek, was a tall man with a thin, high voice and a red face. He used to thrash us.

Our house was in District Five, which is why we went to the school on the edge of town. Most of the pupils were peasant boys. Some of them came barefoot, in smock tops, while others wore long boots and moleskin breeches. I envied them because I had the feeling that they were different from me: tougher and braver. There was one boy called Zöldi who was four or five years older than the rest of us and who kept a penknife tucked inside his boot. One day he showed it to me.

'I'm not even afraid of Almighty God,' he said.

I told my brother this but he didn't believe me.

Our new teacher wasn't interested in making us read or in teaching us to write joined-up like the good old master of the junior year, but he told us a lot of things and made us answer questions. If he caught somebody talking or mucking around in class, he gave them a warning. Then if it happened a second time, he would call the culprit out to the front and quietly say,

'Lie down!'

Then he would address the rest of the class.

'He gets three lashes. Who wants to administer them?'

A great commotion always ensued and ten or fifteen people usually stood up to volunteer. The teacher would look at them each in turn and finally pick one and hand him the cane.

'If you don't use your whole strength,' he said, 'then you'll be next!'

A deathly hush would then fall, while the class watched the caning and listened to the victim's bellows. Everybody admired the boys who didn't make a sound and who never cried, but I noticed that everybody hated them a little bit as well. I thought a lot about why this should be but I was never able to explain it.

I was never worried about being caned. I knew that the teacher would take into account the fact that my father was an army Major and that he had a sharp sword, so he would never dare to have me thrashed.

The teacher soon realised that Zöldi was the best at manipulating the cane. From that time on, it was always Zöldi who administered the thrashings. He was masterful at it. He even held the cane differently from everybody else. Hardly a lesson went by without one or two thrashings taking place. There were some warm, golden autumn afternoons when the whole class was restless and fidgety and on days like that the entire second lesson, from three to four o'clock, was taken up with canings. Every second bench had a boy sitting on it hunched and blubbing.

Once my nose started bleeding and I was allowed to go down to get some water from the cloakroom attendant. The nosebleed soon stopped and I was just going back upstairs, when on the ground floor corridor—the girls' corridor—I saw Little Emma. She was standing at the classroom door, facing it. But she soon noticed me. It was obvious that she had been sent out. I went up to her. I would have liked to give her a kiss and comfort her somehow, but then I noticed that she was not in the least bit sorry. We didn't say anything, we just looked at each other. She was so sweet and proud. It was as if she wanted me to remember that my father might be a Major but hers was a Lieutenant Colonel. She reached for her plait, undid its pink ribbon and began re-tying it. I watched her doing this, completely calmly, but every so often she looked up at me and then I felt my heart begin to thud.

The following afternoon, when she came round to our house, she secretly asked me not to tell anyone that she had been sent out of the classroom. I didn't. But that evening I did ask Irma what Emma had been punished for.

'None of your business.' That was her answer.

Irma was loathsome. At that moment, I would gladly have beaten her to a pulp. She was jealous of Emma. She did not want me to love Emma or Emma to love me. She never let me get near her. She stuck close by her side, hugging her and kissing her and talking baby talk. She always make sure I never got a chance to talk to her. She would call her over, link arms and walk off with her to the far end of the garden. It left me feeling very bitter.

But then, suddenly, the great friendship ended in a huge tiff. One day, I noticed that they had stopped coming out of school together and were each leaving with a different girl. Emma stopped coming round to our house, too. I kept pestering my sister with questions, asking why they had quarrelled, but she just turned her back on me and ran away. To get my revenge, at supper time, I told Father what she had done but she stayed stubbornly silent under his questioning, which led to her being made to go and kneel in the corner and not being allowed an apple.

Weeks went by. In vain I tried to persuade my sister to make up with Emma but she just continued with her stubborn silence. Her eyes were full of tears though, and more than once I heard her crying in bed.

Around the middle of October, a terrible thing happened at school. Our teacher tried to have Zöldi thrashed. He called him up to the front.

'Come over here!'

But Zöldi did not move.

Then the order rang out: 'Bring him over to me!'

Ten or fifteen boys rushed at him from the benches near the back. Many of them were boys who were afraid of Zöldi or who had a grudge against him. I hated him too and I can't deny that my first instinct was to join the boys who were dragging him up to the front, but then it suddenly occurred to me that my father would certainly despise me if he found out that I had joined forces with so many against just one. So I stayed where I was, holding my breath. I could feel my knees trembling. The boys were panting as they tackled Zöldi. They tried to push him off the bench. Some of them grabbed his feet, which he had hooked onto the bar underneath. Others tried to loosen his fingers, which were gripping the edge of the seat. It took at least five minutes to move him. At last they managed to knock him to the floor. He still clung on but did not dare to lash out, probably because he thought that the teacher, who was standing on his chair to watch the battle, would intervene. Szladek's face was brick-red with rage.

At last they managed to get hold of Zöldi by both arms and legs. They lugged him over to Szladek's podium, his back scraping the floor.

'Don't drop him!' shouted Szladek shrilly. 'Lie him on his front and hold his hands and feet.'

Using all their strength, the boys did as they were told. Zöldi now had nothing to hang on to. Boys were kneeling on his hands. Four others were sitting on his feet and two were holding his head down. The teacher had him where he wanted him. Calmly he stooped down, repositioning the boys so that none of them should be hit by the cane, and then set to work, administering five or six lashes in succession. The sound of those lashes was chilling. Rasping, strident, harsh. I broke out in a cold sweat but even so, some irresistible impulse made me stand on tiptoe so as not to miss anything. Szladek had finished. Zöldi did not give so much as a peep.

'Will you continue to be disobedient?' Szladek asked quietly.

'Answer me!' he thundered after a short silence, almost overcome with fury.

But Zöldi did not answer.

'Very well, my boy,' the teacher hissed between his teeth, 'very well indeed. It is all the same to me whether you answer now or later!' With that he set to work again. He had gone completely wild, his strokes were getting faster and faster. He was a big man and he brought all his strength to bear. By the end, he was groaning with his exertions. Finally, worn out, he subsided, and asked again in a hoarse, panting voice,

'Will you continue to be disobedient?'

But Zöldi still didn't answer.

Szladek mopped his brow and began again, more slowly this time. After every lash he paused, and each time he paused he asked the same question:

'Will you continue to be disobedient?'

It went on like this ten or fifteen more times. At last a hideous cry was heard.

'No-o-o!'

Szladek put down the cane and sent the boys back to their places. Zöldi hauled himself to his feet, adjusted the parts of his clothing that had come awry in the struggles and went back to his seat. His nose and cheeks were covered in dirt from the classroom floor. Tears dropped onto his jacket. He spat blood.

But the teacher called him out to the front once more.

'Did anyone give you permission to go back to your seat? Come here!'

Hanging his head, Zöldi staggered to the front. Szladek, as was customary after a job well done, rubbed his hands and said, in a falsely gentle and benevolent voice,

'I did this to you, dear boy, so that you might take good note and learn for the future. Being disobedient to your teacher is a sign of ingratitude and since I have detected this negative tendency in you, I must give you a little correction.'

The 'little', however, turned into 'a lot' because Szladek then began slapping Zöldi's face, and so warmed to his task that he slapped him and slapped him until Zöldi collapsed against the wall. He managed to steady himself and then turned and just ran out of the room. Szladek swore under his breath, slammed the door—which Zöldi had left open—went back to his podium and sat down. The classroom was so silent you could have heard a fly buzzing.

I had hardly got home that afternoon when I developed a fever which turned delirious. I was put straight to bed and that evening my father asked me a lot of questions. I had to tell him all about what had happened at school. My parents said Szladek was a beast and a monster and made up their minds to find a new teacher for me. A week later, I was sent to the school in the centre of town. I no longer saw Little Emma every day. I thought my heart would break.

On the 25th of October, I read a story in the newspaper about a coachman who had been hanged for robbing and murdering one of his passengers. There was a long description about how the coachman had behaved in prison and at the gallows on the morning of his execution. That evening, at supper, my parents discussed the hanging and Father told us about a hanging that he had seen twenty years before.

'I would love to have seen that!' I cried.

'Be thankful that you didn't,' said Father, 'and never go

and see another, because it will give you nightmares for seven years, as it did to me.'

The following afternoon, after school, I suggested to my brother Gábor that we build a gallows and hang a cat or a dog. Gábor was taken with the idea and soon we were hard at work in the attic. We used a piece of washing line for the rope and tied a noose at the end. Making the gallows itself was more difficult, though. Firstly because we did not have a plank of wood and secondly because we were worried that if we started building a gallows in the garden, our parents would make a fuss.

Gábor was not an enthusiastic torturer of animals but once he embarked on something, he had wonderful ideas. Last year, for example, he chopped a live cat in half with the big kitchen knife. That happened in the garden. Anni and Juci caught the cat, then we all held it down, spread-eagled on its back. Gábor sliced it across the belly with the kitchen knife.

We slung the rope over one of the beams in the attic. That same afternoon, a dachshund wandered into our garden from the street. We shut the gate, caught the dog and soon we were all up in the attic. The girls squealed with excitement. Gábor and I calmly made preparations.

'You are the judge,' pronounced Gábor, 'and I am the executioner. You have to tell me when everything is ready for the execution.'

'Very well,' I said. 'Executioner, do your duty.'

Gábor pulled on the rope while I held the dog off the ground. Then, when my brother gave the sign, I let it go. The dachshund let out dismal, deep whining sounds and scrabbled at the air with its yellow and black legs. But then suddenly it stretched out and was still. We looked at it for a while, then left it hanging and went down for tea. After tea, the girls hung around the gate and tempted another dog into the garden with sugar lumps. They took it to Gábor for another execution but my brother waved the idea away, announcing that one hanging was enough for one day. So Juci opened the gate and let the dog go.

During the days that followed, we completely forgot about our gallows because we got a new ball. Gábor and I spent all our time playing Sevensies. After that we talked about Emma. Gábor announced that he hated her because she was so stuck up and said it was idiotic the way Irma kept imploring her to make friends again.

'It would be a good thing if they never made up, so she would never come back here again with her airs and graces!' said Gábor angrily.

But Gábor's wish was not granted. The following afternoon Emma turned up at our house. She came with Irma.

'Loathsome!' whispered Gábor.

'Sweet and lovely!' I said to myself, but I was very annoyed with Irma.

Irma, meanwhile, was floating on air. All the time we were playing, she kept going over to Emma, hugging her and kissing her. But later on they started quarrelling again.

'I thought you promised you would never speak to Rosie again,' said Irma, almost in tears.

'I never said any such thing!' said Emma stoutly, and simpered.

Juci and Anni started whispering together. Gábor, Irma and I looked at Little Emma. How pretty she was! How pretty!

It was a beautiful sunny afternoon, one of the last days of autumn. The garden was all ours. Mother and Father had gone out riding. Cook brought us coffee, then went into the kitchen to make the supper.

'Have you ever seen a hanging?' my sister asked Emma when we had finished our tea.

'No!' said Emma, and shook her head so that her golden curls bounced round her face.

'But you know what it is? You've heard your papa talking about it.'

'Yes, he said a murderer had been hanged,' said Emma coolly, without interest.

'Well, we've got a gallows,' said Juci proudly.

And so saying, we all piled up to the attic to show Emma a hanging. Gábor and I had buried the dachshund a few days ago, in the compost heap. The rope was hanging free.

'Let's play at hanging,' said Irma. 'Emma will be the criminal. We'll hang her.'

'No! *You!*' giggled Emma.

'Executioner, do your duty!' Gábor commanded.

Little Emma went pale but she was still smiling.

'Stand perfectly still,' said Irma.

I hung the noose around Emma's neck.

'No! I don't want to do this!' protested Emma.

'The accused is pleading for mercy!' said Gábor, rather red in the face, 'but the assistant executioners have seized the condemned woman.'

Juci and Anni had taken hold of Emma's arms.

'No!' screamed Emma. 'No, I won't let you!' And she burst into tears.

'Mercy comes from God alone!' intoned Gábor.

Irma grasped her friend by the knees and held her aloft. Emma was too heavy though, and Irma almost fell, so I went over and helped her. It was the first time I had held Emma in my arms. My brother pulled on the rope, wound the end of it round a beam and tied it fast. Emma swung in the air. At first she waved her arms and kicked out with her thin little white-stockinged legs. They were so funny, the movements she made. I couldn't see her face because it was quite dark in the attic. But then the movements just suddenly stopped. Her body hung straight down, as if she was searching for a stool, something to stand on, with her toes. After that she went completely still. A sickly panic gripped all of us. We tumbled headlong down from the attic and hid in different parts of the garden. Anni and Juci ran home.

It was Cook who found the body, when she went up to the attic for something half an hour later. She called Emma's father over, before Mother and Father got home…

The diary entry ends there. The diarist, whose misfortune it was to have played a part in this horrific scene, can tell us no more about it. All I know of the family is that their father, the Major, now rests in peace. Irma is a widow and Gábor an army officer.

A kis Emma. Published posthumously

Cécile Tormay

THE GOLDEN SNAKE

He put down his pen and leaned back in his chair. He had been labouring at this his whole life long. And now, the great *oeuvre* was complete. All those years ago, when he had first begun looking forward to this moment, he had imagined it would be attended by far more fanfare. Yet now the moment had come, and everything around him seemed as shabby as ever. Shabby and unchanged. The clock still ticked on the wall. The table lamp still smoked as it always had done. Outwardly, nothing seemed to have happened at all, and yet—and yet the great work was finished. He had just completed the tenth and final volume of *The Decline and Fall of Egypt*.

An old, familiar sensation seemed to stir beneath his skin. A smile was trying to burst forth from somewhere deep within, from somewhere in the depths of his soul. But his face was as dry and wrinkled as old parchment and his features, schooled so long in stillness, had forgotten how to do it.

He had been a young man when he had first made his bargain with Truth and Knowledge, contracted himself with Science—with his own reputation. Since that day, he had worked fanatically, zealously hard.

He had trodden every ruin of the wide and secretive valley of the Nile. He had searched each crevice of the rock tombs of Thebes. He had compelled the royal tablets of Abydos to divulge the secrets of the ages in a modern tongue. He had interpreted inscriptions on obelisks, deciphered hieroglyphs on temple walls. He had gleaned wisdom from shards of adamantine granite, from scrolls of papyrus as delicate as a moth's wings.

His hair was already grey by the time he brought his findings, like a hoard of stolen treasure, back to the remote, dusty, silent town of his birth. The days were longer and more unbroken there than elsewhere. And there, completely undisturbed, he had applied the algebra of science to history, unravelling the true cause of the fall of Egypt.

In Volume I, he had wrested the veil of superstition from the enigmatic face of the Egypt of prehistory. In Volume II, he had exploded the shepherds' fairy tales of the Hyksos period. And then—furiously, mercilessly—he had done battle with the incantations and idolatries of millennia. Systematically, down the dynasties, he had peeled away the painted faces of divinity from golden-wrapped mummies. He had reduced to a human scale the superhuman shades of Ramesses and the pharaohs of Sais and Bubastis. He had slain and laid to rest the myths of Actium and Alexandria.

At the merest touch of his methods and his learning, the legends died away and mythology retreated. All that was left was cool, clear fact. Ruins, bones and tombs. Disdainfully he proved, in Volume VII, that the humiliating passion which had reduced the great Mark Antony to a gibbering hysteric, in thrall to the degenerate Cleopatra, was no more than a readily diagnosable medical psychosis. He devoted the final three volumes to demonstrating that the long decline of the empire of the pharaohs is attributable simply to an immutable natural law that governs the spring and fall of all things.

It was a seminal work, this thing that he had just completed. He had applied his theory precisely and clinically to thirty-one Egyptian dynasties; carried it unsullied through ten folio volumes. It was true that all this had taken up a good deal of time, but after all…

With weary tenderness, he looked down at his manuscript and then—as if expecting recognition to come from some quarter—looked shyly around the four walls of his musty study.

Under the light of the paraffin lamp, muted by its glass shade, the barren armchairs yawned cavernously. No one had ever sat in them. Worn and dog-eared works of reference stared expressionlessly at him from the sagging bookshelves. He had plundered their contents long ago. He had no further use for them.

Suddenly, he felt enveloped by a peculiar sense of emptiness. It was an emptiness that emanated from within him and spread outwards across his writing desk…

A faint, nervous question began to stumble towards the forefront of his mind. What will I do tomorrow? Tomorrow, and the day after that? The sense of emptiness began to grow stronger. The musty couch, the chairs, the bookshelves began to gnaw at him. There was nothing here but him and the furniture. He opened the door and went out into the hall. Suddenly, the old professor was aware that there was no one there, either. Not in the hallway. Not in the town. Not anywhere.

The sense of emptiness grew and grew, devouring space and distance until suddenly it was everywhere. Everywhere his mind turned, he found nothing but a gaping void.

For the first time in his life, he was aware of being alone.

His features took on a curious expression, as if he was pondering something. Solitude is essential for work, he thought. But for other things? Now, for instance, he ought to feel happy but instead he was filled with a furtive unease. The mortal frame that had stood up from his chair was stiff from sitting so long.

His chair creaked. The floorboards groaned. He began to pace up and down. Once again, he poked his head into the hallway. Instantly, he drew it back. He opened the window. He was scarcely aware that he had done so. He sat back at his desk and fixed the door with his beady, barely blinking, bird-like eyes.

Why was he looking at the door? Who did he think would possibly come in? He had long buried his father and mother. He had never had friends. And as for women... His only acquaintance with them was in the form of golden-brown Egyptian queens, long since dead and gone.

He knitted his brow, as if trying to bring distant, indistinct landscapes into focus. Someone came to his mind... He had been a mere schoolboy at the time. Raw and adolescent longings had kept him awake at night. The acacia trees had been in blossom and the great Egyptologist had written a lot of terrible poems. But a good many years had gone by since then. The children in the little town had long ago begun to refer to him as the 'Old Professor'. And slowly, mournfully, in the next street along, a girl with beautiful chestnut hair had grown old.

And then, from the end of that very street, above the clustering tiled roofs, the bell in the tall church tower began to chime. The old professor did not count how many hours it struck. What difference did it make to him? It was only telling the time. Time, a phenomenon which was passing. Had perhaps already passed.

A shelf creaked. The lamp sputtered. The flame chased round and round its burned-out wick. It flickered, it sparked. Then all at once it was gone.

The old professor was left in the dark. Testily, he fumbled for a box of matches. As he did so, he knocked something over, a small object buried under the heaped-up mass of his notes. His hand made contact with the smooth, cool contours of a little clay pot. Who knew how long it had been on his desk? The pot was a repository of odds and ends; it was filled with small fragments of antiquity. He looked closer. He could make out the pot's shape, its colour, and, spilling from its neck, a whole jumble of precious artefacts. Suddenly, it was as if he could see in the dark and he didn't understand how this could be. Nervously, he looked over his shoulder. From outside, between the acacia boughs that waved against the iron window bars, a pale, wan shaft of moonlight cast itself into the room. He turned back to see its silvery light shining on his desk like vapour.

The old professor bent his head. By the moonlight, he began inspecting his cache of antiquities. His mighty manuscript was suddenly strewn with stone scarabs, with linen shreds of mummy wrapping, with green-glazed terracotta idols, all of them thousands of years old. And in among them was a beaten gold bracelet in the shape of a snake.

All this had been in… He shook his head. No, it dated from well before that. It was over thirty years ago. In Luxor— or was it Abu Simbel? He had brought the clay pot back from somewhere near there. And the snake bracelet with the golden scales? Yes, he remembered now. He had bought it from a camel driver at the foot of the Sphinx at Giza. And since then, he had never found the time to make a scientific calculation of its age or its antiquarian value.

For an instant, he felt gripped by the urge to light the lamp, to take out his magnifying glass; but he did not move. The urge gave way to a sense of unfamiliar but welcome lassitude. Strangely numbed and disarmed, he sat still and rested, as if absolved of all further responsibility, as if detached from everything. Until now, his head had been filled with cogs, joined to one another by belts, which made them turn and which drove them onwards. But now, those belts had worked themselves loose or had fallen slack. The cogs were turning of their own accord, humming and spinning, but to no purpose. And it was good.

At the open window, a wind got up, a nervous, fitful wind that tossed the acacia boughs to and fro. With it, it brought the scents and smells of spring, the fragrance of green things. It was as if flower meadows were suddenly sailing over the town, forests and mountain streams, damp furrows of ploughed earth.

The acacia branches waved against the window bars. The

moonlight danced across the writing desk. The old professor began to take deep, rapid breaths. Suddenly, his heart seemed to skip a beat. It was as if the cogs in his brain had begun to turn backwards, zanily out of control. The feeling only lasted for a minute; he could not bear to analyse it further. Everything around him seemed blown awry. As if the moonlight and the scents on the night breeze had freshened everything with a sudden shaft of air…

Moonlight—that old deceiver! He did not allow himself to pursue the idea further. But still, he shifted position, so as not to be in the direct path of the moonbeam's lambent glow. In doing so, he somehow seemed to dazzle his eyes. The golden scales on the snake's slender body began to rise up and bristle. As if curled on its nest, it spread itself in an arc across his great history of the pharaohs. It held its flat little head erect. Its jasper eyes glittered, as if they could see.

The professor could not stop staring at it. And as he did so, the little Nile snake seemed to join with the moonlight in a kind of mystic supplication, recalling Myth and Legend back from exile. In vain did the brain of the old professor squirm and protest. It was not the Cleopatra of his book that he found himself imagining, but the other Cleopatra. A Cleopatra who rose naked before his eyes, godlike under a clinging, silvery veil. Nearer and nearer she came, until suddenly, there she stood, in all her glory, an apparition straight out of the myth he believed he had slain and laid to rest, a dream of an Egyptian queen whose devouring, inflammatory kisses on the lips of Antony had for a brief moment caused the known world to hold its breath.

The beady, bird-like eyes of the old man gave a startled blink, as if he was suddenly looking into an unfamiliar, hypnotic light. The golden snake had made itself master over Egypt's ten-volume *Decline and Fall*… But it was only for a moment. The moment passed and the professor ceased to marvel. Suddenly, he was filled with anxious worry. What if the old myths were real after all? What if his newly completed book were mere hallucination? What if the true story of Egypt lay not in the natural laws of extinction and decay but in the burgeoning of youth and lust and love?

He buried his head in his hands, as if trying to shore up his tottering theory of senescence, preventing it from being dashed to the ground. Between his knotted fingers, his head began to tremble pathetically and his poor old eyes turned desperately towards the door, as if waiting for someone to come in who would pronounce a final verdict.

But there was nothing. Only the sense of emptiness he had felt before. And he had nobody. Not one person in the world. He closed his eyes and heaved a sigh. He had taken many wrong turns in his life. What if those same wrong turns were mirrored in his work? Vaguely, somewhere in his mind, it occurred to him that both in life and in his work he had run a blade through mystery and fable. Neither his life nor his work had a heart…

And just at that moment, the wind blew the window shut. The old professor shook himself and opened his eyes. The moonlight had slanted away from the writing desk. And now, with the window closed, he could smell nothing more than the familiar, comforting must and mildew, the smell that emanated from the pages of the white manuscript, his great work, *The Decline and Fall of Egypt*. The little golden snake was nothing more than a piece of lifeless archaeology.

The old professor rubbed his eyes, as if to rid himself of the after-effects of a demented dream. He felt a little ashamed of himself. He looked to right, then left. He coughed, he cleared his throat. Then he dropped the golden snake perfunctorily back into the clay pot. He turned his mind to other things, to the task of indexing his ten-volume *magnum opus*. To immortality.

Az egyiptomi aranykígyó. 1918

László Tóth

MINISTRY OF JUSTICE

The corridor was still empty. Above its broad swathe of red carpet, the morning light was causing little motes of golden dust to dance. It was early: half past nine. The place was deserted except for a pair of ushers, their whiskers carefully curled, who loitered by the entrance to the side corridor.

Kelemen was the first to arrive. As he pushed open the glass doors, he stood perceptibly straighter and instinctively reached up to adjust his necktie. Then he took out his gold-rimmed monocle, wiped it carefully on his handkerchief, and fixed it into his right eye. At the end of the corridor, the tall figure of the Serjeant-at-Arms came into view swift and resolute as he made his way towards the Prime Minister's Office. When he saw Kelemen, he gave a cheery greeting.

'You're in early today, I see, Honourable Member.'

He placed particular emphasis on those last two words, but then hurried on his way without waiting for an answer. Despite this, Kelemen was gratified by the greeting, although he knew—oh, how well!—that it was a long time since he had qualified to be addressed in those terms. Steeling himself not to notice the hint of mockery in the Serjeant's tone, he said casually, 'Well, today's a big day.' Then he turned and sauntered off down the corridor to the left, where a couple of people had begun to gather.

Kelemen felt completely at home in this environment, a place where the temperature was carefully contrived to stay the same, winter and summer, so that in winter it felt warm, in summer cool. There was an atmosphere of deliberate hush, broken only occasionally by some spark of altercation at the junction of one of the corridors, or perhaps in front of the Press gallery. Refreshed, even rejuvenated, by the long summer recess, Kelemen wandered up and down under the brightly painted vaults, as calmly and as confidently as if he were indeed still a Member of Parliament.

And yet… That had been a long time ago. A very long time ago! Was it twenty, perhaps…? No, it was better not to count the years. But how glorious it had been, in the days when throngs of young MPs and newspapermen had crowded round him, all eager to know his views. And he had given them chapter and verse, peppering his language with subtle, French-style *aperçus*, with murderous little barbed asides and sober, punctilious legalese. And when he went into the chamber, the ladies in the upper gallery all whispered to each other:

'Who is that tall, handsome, dark-haired man? There— the one in the frock-coat, with the monocle?'

'Do you really not know? It's Kelemen Lontay, the cleverest speech-maker on the Opposition bench. He has the ear of the Party leader.'

It was completely true. That distinguished old gentleman, the Party leader, had never done anything without consulting Kelemen, especially after his health began to fail. There were only two people who were completely in his confidence. Sándor, his secretary, and Kelemen.

It had been a different world in those days. A world where people still respected knowledge and experience, where they still appreciated a cultural education. Not like today… With an air of disdain, Kelemen surveyed the corridor, acknowledged an elderly reporter's greeting with a supercilious nod. The reporter went up to him, just like reporters had always done in the old days. But now, it was only this single old has-been who approached him.

'What is your opinion of the situation, Honourable Member?'

He still seemed interested in Kelemen's views. The trouble was, it was a good ten years since he had been attached to any newspaper. Instead, he had taken to hanging around the corridors, a thin, shrunken figure, whispering little scraps of information into people's ears, scraps that always amounted to the same thing, namely that old Kobich—who had once, briefly, been Justice Minister and then, for a month or two, Speaker of the House—was coming up to Budapest and then… But nobody took any notice of him.

Now he and Kelemen stood side by side in front of one of the windows, like ghostly shades of a bygone era.

The well-known leader of the left-wing walked past them, his squat figure radiating determination, his face very serious. It was clear that he was scanning the crowd for someone.

'Hello, Gábor,' said Kelemen in a lofty voice. 'Who are you looking for?'

But the other man scarcely acknowledged him. He

inclined his head and hurried on his way without replying.

Kelemen swallowed hard. Unconscionable! How rude! And to think that the world now belonged to that lot! Things were very different in our day. That man was still in a romper suit when I...

Yes. When Kelemen had toured the country, borne aloft on his supporters' shoulders. When he had paraded down flag-lined streets, strewn with flowers, 'Long live Kelemen Lontay, our candidate for the Party of Independence and 1848!' What an election that had been! In the winter of 1905, when he had defeated the old general in that northern mining town. When they had sent old Fejérváry packing, him and his guardsmen's government[24]! And when, up at the palace, he had personally told the Emperor that...

Kelemen turned away from the ageing, out-to-pasture old newshound and looked out of the window at the Danube. A lot of water has certainly flowed under those bridges since then, he sighed to himself. And ever since then, in this new world we live in...

Ever since then, he had never managed to repeat that success. He had stood for election to the first national assembly, in his old seat. He had lost. Some footling little civil servant had beaten him by a thousand votes. He had stood again in the second election, and again in the third one, too. And after that he had given up. Why bother? Any money he had had had long since evaporated. And he had to admit that his legal practice was delivering rather modest results. Being able to put 'MP' after the director's name had certainly not been bad for business. But now...!

Large clouds were massing above the Buda Hills, scudding across the sky.

'According to old Kobich,' said the ageing hack, with a wink, 'our time is coming. He thinks this is just a temporary aberration. He has grand plans.' He leaned closer to Kelemen and whispered: 'He's got you earmarked for Permanent Under-Secretary for Justice.'

'Me? Really?' Kelemen seemed momentarily lost for words. 'Oh, but it's not possible. After all, the old boy will be in for a post…'

But he was just saying that. He didn't really believe it. Permanent Under-Secretary for Justice, though—that was something! And he deserved it, too. It was only thanks to the vilest skulduggery that he'd been held back during the coalition… But if he had… If the old goat had trusted him more, well, things would have been very different. Though who knows? Perhaps it was better… Yes, it was definitely better that it hadn't happened. He had been too young. But now… Now, when there were so many complex, sensitive issues at stake, now was the time when his brand of legal expertise could really come into its own. All the subtle wiliness he had built up over the years. Because after all, he was sixty-two—no, sixty-one years old. And this had been on the cards before, ten years ago. The newspapers had all predicted it, the Party leader had said that it would get the green light if… But then, out of nowhere, the Press chief had… No, no, it was much for the best that he had played no role in that particular administration. Now, though, it was imperative to get the Justice Minister's attention. How fortunate that he had come here today! No decision had yet been made about the Permanent Under-Secretary position. Not that he would be able to bring the subject up now, of course, not after the Prime Minister's policy speech. But tomorrow or the day after. It would be worth having a word with that boy Jenő, that fellow who had once been his legal clerk. Jenő was very thick with the Minister. Yes, he'd look out for him later.

By now, the corridor was beginning to fill up. People were standing around arguing in little groups. Reporters and minutes-takers were scurrying hither and thither.

One of the Opposition leaders, a man who had formerly been Prime Minister, suddenly detached himself from one of the groups and came over to where Kelemen was standing and drew him into an embrace.

'Good to see you, Kelemen old boy, it's been a long time! I'm glad you dropped in today. Very opportune as it happens, because...'

He couldn't get to the end of his sentence, because just then someone from the Prime Minister's office came over and whispered something in his ear.

'Yes, Sir... His Excellency...' were the only words that Kelemen caught.

The former Prime Minister abruptly shook Kelemen's hand. 'Terribly sorry, old boy. I'll be straight back. It's just that I'm wanted by...' And he hurried off without finishing his sentence.

Kelemen found himself beginning to wonder. What was going on? Was something afoot? That former PM wasn't a man who usually had much time for him, but now, suddenly, all this business about how opportune it was that he was here. And then he had hurried off, saying he was wanted by… Could it have been the Justice Minister? Oh, nonsense, for Heaven's sake! It was most unlikely. It was just that… He had spoken to him so particularly. There had been something about the way he had emphasised that word 'opportune'…

A smooth-chinned young columnist came sidling up to Kelemen.

'Heard any gossip?'

Kelemen couldn't stand this fellow. And with good reason. The previous winter, he had gone up to the Press gallery, just at a time when there had been a lot going on, the whole House completely thronged, and this little pipsqueak had pertly asked him what he was doing up there. Him, Kelemen Lontay, who had been going up there for the past twenty years! Entirely by long-established right. And then this fresh-faced little twerp had said he was sorry, but only journalists were allowed into the gallery. To which Kelemen had airily riposted that he was a former Member of Parliament, a remark which had elicited the flippant reply, 'Well, why don't you shuffle off to the former Houses of Parliament, then?' Yet now, here was this same wretched brat sidling up to him! Extraordinary!

The ageing, out-to-pasture old reporter put his hand on his younger colleague's shoulder.

'The Honourable gentleman is not at liberty to speak, though he would certainly have a story for you!'

The young columnist looked at Kelemen inquiringly.

'I'm sorry, but I can't say anything just yet,' said Kelemen, lingering meaningfully over the 'just yet'.

'What I *can* tell you, though,' the ageing reporter went on, 'is that intricate discussions are currently underway about the Permanent Under-Secretary for Justice post. A post which the Honourable Gentleman, if he so wished…'

'Please, please, no more of this,' said Kelemen.

He left them to it.

Ten minutes later, another of his newspaper acquaintances came up to him and asked him if it was true that he was being tipped for Permanent Under-Secretary for Justice.

Kelemen felt a little ruffled and said, 'Please, let us not discuss it.' But then, half an hour later, a cabinet secretary drew him into a corner and began muttering something about a notary public. Was this yet another person who seemed to know something?

And then the bell went and everyone flooded into the chamber.

'You're not coming in?' asked the cabinet secretary.

'No, perhaps a bit later,' said Kelemen, flustered.

Where should he go, though? Into the chamber? Certainly not to the Press gallery. He didn't want a repeat of that infamous incident.

After a quarter of an hour, he made his way up to the clerks' gallery and it was from there that he heard the Prime Minister make his policy speech.

Well expressed, pithy, meaty and bold, he thought to himself. This man is here to stay.

He looked across to where the cabinet members were sitting. The Justice Minister seemed quietly absorbed in what the Prime Minister had to say. But then suddenly, he looked up and scanned the galleries. And when his gaze reached the clerks' gallery, he seemed to pause for a moment, as if he had picked a face out from the crowd, and his eye came to rest on it, fixedly. But whose face? Could it be Kelemen he was looking at? Yes, he definitely seemed to be looking in Kelemen's direction. Kelemen smiled and nodded—and the Justice Minister nodded back!

He nodded back! It wasn't a coincidence, surely? But for Heaven's sake, they had known each other for some time. Two gentlemen exchanging glances, what of it? There was no point trying to read anything into it.

But all the same, Kelemen's heart began to beat a little faster.

The policy speech was over. The applause went on and on. It seemed that it would never die down, certainly not on the right-hand side of the chamber. But plenty of applause was coming from the left as well. Then the congratulations began. People began to crowd round the speaker.

It was at that point that the Justice Minister stood up, picked up his briefcase and slowly began to make his way out of the chamber. People were starting to drift away from the clerks' gallery, too. Kelemen among them. A reporter came over to him.

'What is your opinion of the speech we just heard, Sir?'

'It was well expressed, pithy and bold.' Kelemen reiterated his verdict, this time out loud. 'The Prime Minister is clearly a man of immense ability. I am someone with a great deal of parliamentary experience,'—and here he drew himself up fully erect—'and as such, I feel bound to say that I hardly remember a more impressive policy speech than this one. I am confident that we are looking at a stable and long-term administration.' Obligingly, he shook the reporter's hand and made his way towards the members' corridor.

He had hardly gone five paces when he saw the Justice Minister coming towards him.

'I'm so glad to have bumped into you,' said the Minister. 'I've been wanting to talk to you for days, old chap.'

'My pleasure, I'm sure…'

The Justice Minister took him by the elbow and led him off into an alcove. They sat down. Kelemen realised that people were beginning to notice them. That snotty-nosed young columnist was one of them.

'I was just wondering,' the Minister said, 'if you might be prepared to accept…'

Kelemen closed his eyes, suddenly overcome with the thought that he might be about to die of happiness.

'You were wondering, Minister?' he stuttered. He could hardly get his words out.

'Yes. I was wondering if you might possibly agree to give my son a bit of coaching for his bar exams. You see, I'd dearly like the boy to shine. But I feel he's a bit shaky on commercial and inheritance law. What he needs is not just someone who can help him get to grips with all the complexities, but a man who can teach him how to hold forth about them in a convincing way. And I vividly remember the splendid speeches you used to make…'

But Kelemen no longer heard. He had the sense of a voice coming at him from somewhere a long, long way away, but what it was saying, he had no idea.

The Justice Minister touched his arm and said, raising his voice a little,

'So, may I hope that you'll say yes? I mean, obviously,' he added, in a lowered tone, 'obviously we'll make it worth your while.'

Kelemen shook himself. He fixed his monocle firmly in his eye. He shook his head.

'I am sorry, Sir. I do not operate a kindergarten.' He stood up. 'But if at any time you should need advice on this matter, of course I am always at your service.' With a haughty nod, he held out his hand.

The Justice Minister shook his head and said, with a placid smile, 'I'm sorry. I thought the arrangement would be mutually beneficial.'

Kelemen turned on his heel and quietly walked away. Calm and dignified, with his head erect, once again instinctively reaching up to adjust his necktie, he proceeded down the length of the teeming corridor.

And at that moment he really did look like a Permanent Under-Secretary of the old, pre-War school.

'Well?' said the young columnist, eagerly running up to him.

'I turned it down,' said Kelemen quietly.

And proudly, with his head held high, he continued on his way.

Államtitkárválság. Published 1941

The authors

Short biographical notes on all the writers whose works appear in this book, in alphabetical order.

Endre Ady (1877–1919): 'I am yours in my rage, in my faithlessness, in the agonies of love. Dolefully Magyar...' Ady was a very great, if self-centred writer (he was born with six fingers, which he took to mean that he was a shaman). He came to prominence as a journalist and was published in the first number of *Nyugat* ('*West*'), which appeared in 1908 and which became Hungary's leading literary periodical. Ady was one of its editors and through his output— free-thinking, anti-establishment and vigorously anti-war—he became a figurehead of its early years. Ady was first and foremost a poet. He is less well known as a writer of prose fiction, though he produced some finely crafted stories. He died, following complications from both the Spanish flu and syphilis, at the young age of 41.

Géza Csáth (1887–1919): Csáth was the pen name of József Brenner, a cousin of Dezső Kosztolányi (*see below*), from the city known in Hungarian as Szabadka (now Subotica, Serbia). He studied medicine and his first jobs were in psychiatric hospitals. Much of the dark psychological disturbance of his writings comes from his experiences in this field, as well as from his dabbling with drugs, a habit he became unable to relinquish and which soon led to complete derangement. He shot his wife and took his own life shortly after.

Marie von Ebner-Eschenbach (1830–1916): Of aristocratic ancestry, from Bohemia on her father's side, the young Marie was encouraged in her writing first by her stepmother and later by her husband, a professor of Physics and Chemistry. It was her early love of the theatre that steered her towards the style that suited her talents best: the story-in-letters or novel-in-dialogue. Her themes are gently psychological, digging at contemporary mores but never in an overtly subversive way.

Egid Filek von Wittinghausen (1874–1949): An unassuming man who lived an apparently blameless life as an editor of youth magazines and as a schoolteacher, both in his native Vienna as well as in towns now in the Czech Republic. He was, according to his obituary, 'A typically Austrian phenomenon, with a sense of the magic and poetry of small things.' He also turned his talents to the writing of guidebooks, focusing on the natural beauties of his homeland (the Vienna Woods, the Danube landscapes of the Wachau). Much of his fiction is set in the past, in the days of old Austria-Hungary.

Elek Gozsdu (1849–1919): Born in Hungary, to a family with Macedonian roots, Gozsdu qualified as a lawyer but found the law not to his liking. He turned to journalism, but found the late nights necessitated by the coverage of current affairs not to his liking either, so he returned to his legal practice. As a writer, he was influenced by the works of Turgenev and Dostoevsky and enjoyed themes of distressed and fallen gentry. Never prolific and never ranked in the first tier of Hungarian writers, his output and approach nevertheless belonged to the important late 19th-century roster of prose stylists whose achievements paved the way for the great mould-breakers of the *Nyugat* (*see Endre Ady*) generation.

Hugo von Hofmannsthal (1874–1929): The son of a Vienna bank manager, Hofmannsthal's own interests were a long way away from the world of finance. He went on to become one of the great figures of the Viennese *fin de siècle*, a member, with Arthur Schnitzler, of the radical *Jung-Wien* group of coffee-house intellectuals. Known initially for his poetry and his essays, his career took off when he met the composer Richard Strauss, for whom he provided the libretto for *Elektra*, *Der Rosenkavalier* and other operas. The collapse of Austria-Hungary affected him deeply.

Margit Kaffka (1880–1919): One of the members of the first '*Nyugat*' generation, a group of early 20th-century Hungarian writers who contributed to the greatness of the new periodical of the same name, Kaffka wrote some acclaimed poetry but it is as a short story writer that she is best known. Her style is spare and ambiguous, saying little but suggesting much, taking the lives of women as its main focus. She died of the Spanish flu, in Budapest, and Dezső Kosztolányi gave her funeral oration.

Dezső Kosztolányi (1885–1936): A prolific writer, one of the greatest literary figures in Hungary between the World Wars, Kosztolányi's output includes poetry, short stories, translations and, most importantly, novels. Born in provincial Szabadka (now Subotica, Serbia), he spent almost all his adult life in Budapest, where he was a regular contributor to the literary periodical *Nyugat*. Like so many of his generation, he was profoundly affected by the changes that came about after WWI. Not only was his home town assigned to another country, but the legitimacy of his existence as a writer was called into question. On going to meet Béla Kun, the leader of Hungary's Soviet-style government in 1918, he is reported to have asked: 'And what will become of us writers?' The reply was blunt: 'There will be no need for writers in the new People's Republic. You'll have to learn a trade.' A chain smoker, Kosztolányi died of laryngeal cancer.

Károly Lovik (1874–1915): Budapest-born Lovik was one of the 'little figures, literary pioneers without whom the giants could never have existed'—or so wrote the critic Péter Dérczy. If his father had lived, Lovik would almost certainly have followed the family footsteps and become a lawyer; however,

Lovik Sr died, and his son struck out as a journalist, editing a magazine on hunting and horse-riding—a far cry indeed from the modernist, symbolist, iconoclastic work of the writers whom the literary periodical *Nyugat* kept on its books. Lovik's stories are evocative of the lives of men and women of restricted horizons. He died of a brain haemorrhage.

Kálmán Mikszáth (1847–1910): Born in north Hungary, the young Mikszáth embarked, without enthusiasm, on training for the law. It was not long before he abandoned all pretence of studying and took up a post as editor of a local newspaper. He published his first volume of short stories at the age of 27. Fearing nonetheless that he would always be a pauper, he divorced his wife, hoping by so doing to save her from a life of penury. When his career took off and his fame was assured, he remarried her, and went on to become hugely successful, fêted as a literary lion, in outward appearance the archetypal portly, jovial, cigar-puffing after-dinner *raconteur*. Such was his success that he lived to see his native village, Szklabonya, renamed Mikszáthfalva ('Mikszáthville') in his honour (it is now Sklabiná, Slovakia).

Zsigmond Móricz (1795–1881): Born in east Hungary, a child of the Great Plain, Móricz initially set out to study theology, but like many a young student of his talents and inclinations, he soon took up law, and from that gravitated to journalism. Nothing that he published belonged to the realm of *belles lettres* until he joined the staff of the periodical *Nyugat*, in its first year of publication (1908), and for a time his short stories, together with Ady's poetry, were the most read pieces in the magazine. His first story to be published, *Seven Farthings*, was to make his name and he went on to become a popular novelist and playwright. Politically, Móricz came in for much criticism: initially for supporting the Socialist and Communist revolutions after WWI, and later, as editor of *Nyugat*, for turning his back on old friends whose radical views had made their lives untenable following the collapse of those Socialist and Communist revolutions. Móricz's personal life was similarly complicated.

Therese Rie (1878–1934): Born in Vienna into a non-practising Jewish family, the daughter of a paediatrician, Therese Rie began working as an opera and theatre critic and later, after the death of her husband, turned full-time to fiction, publishing under the pen name L. Andro. She wrote novels and short stories and was also an accomplished translator from French.

Rainer Maria Rilke (1875–1926): Rilke was born and brought up in Prague, to parents who seem to have been unaware of their son's needs and inclinations. Mourning the death of a daughter, they dressed him in girl's clothing; later, despite his clearly sensitive nature, they enrolled him in a military academy. When finally old enough to make his own decisions, Rilke studied art history, literature and philosophy at university. He led a peripatetic life, in Russia, Munich, the Worpswede artists' colony in north Germany (where he met his wife, the artist Clara Westhoff), Paris (where he worked as Rodin's secretary) and finally Switzerland, where he died of leukaemia. Although Rilke wrote both short stories and a novel, he is best known for his poetry, which is some of the most beautiful and evocative in the German language. His poem cycle *Das Stundenbuch* (*Book of Hours*) was greatly admired by Dezső Kosztolányi. His friendship with Princess Marie von Thurn and Taxis led to a sojourn in her castle outside Trieste, where he wrote his famous *Duino Elegies*.

Alexander Roda Roda (1872–1945): Born Šandor Rosenfeld, in a town now in the Czech Republic, Roda Roda spent most of his life in Osijek, in present-day Croatia. His pen name, which in Croatian translates as 'Stork Stork', originated in his early years, when he and his sister Marie wrote jointly under the double pen name of Roda Roda (it is said that the siblings enjoyed watching the storks nesting on the roof of their house). Alexander dropped out of law school and enlisted as a soldier, though he was dismissed from the army following breaches of the officers' code. However, he was given an official position as a war reporter during WWI. When the war ended, he turned in earnest to writing. His output included plays (he was also a keen actor and would sport a red waistcoat he had had made from the lining of his army coat), stories and novels, mostly in a humorous vein. In 1933, he wrote a satire attacking Hitler. When the Nazis annexed Austria in 1938, he fled to

Switzerland, from where he emigrated to the United States, after the Swiss refused to let him stay. 'The most aggressive form of warfare,' he later wrote, 'is the taking up of a position of neutrality.' His sister Marie died in 1935. His other sister, a doctor, was murdered in the Holocaust.

Joseph Roth (1894–1939): Born near Lemberg (now Lviv, Ukraine), Roth studied literature in Vienna, fought in WWI and then, after Hitler came to power, left Austria for exile in Paris. In many ways, the lives and careers of Roth and Stefan Zweig were intertwined. Both were Austrian Jews whose whole lives and chief subject matter had been bound up with the multi-ethnic Empire they loved and whose disintegration affected them so deeply. Roth's best known work is *The Radetzky March*, in which the Empire is very much the protagonist, an entity which he views through a soft and nostalgic lens, as a place where people of different creeds and callings could live harmoniously side by side, tolerant of difference. The ensuing disasters in Roth's homeland, as well as failures in his personal life, drove him to alcoholism. He collapsed in the Café Tournon, near the Jardin du Luxembourg, and died in hospital.

Richard Schaukal (1874–1942): Born in Brünn, Moravia (now Brno, Czech Republic), Schaukal studied law and then took up a career in government administration, which culminated in his being ennobled by Emperor Karl, the last

of the Habsburgs, in 1918. Thereafter, Schaukal devoted himself to literature, writing prolifically, both in prose and verse. He cultivated an extensive circle of literary and artistic acquaintance, among whom were Rilke, Marie von Ebner-Eschenbach and Arthur Schnitzler. Schaukal's best known work, his *Life and Opinions of Andreas Balthesser*, subtly satirises the figure of the world-weary dandy, idly and elegantly disdainful of the very society that sustains him.

Arthur Schnitzler (1862–1931): Schnitzler's doctor father disapproved of his son's ambition to write. He also despaired of the young man's ardent nature. Finding that the 16-year-old Arthur had slept with a prostitute, he presented him with an illustrated tract on venereal disease. Dutifully, Schnitzler took a degree in medicine in Vienna, but he was never able to take the profession seriously. He wrote stories and plays, frequented the coffee houses, was a member of the modernist group *Jung-Wien* and befriended Freud, who considered Schnitzler his 'double', doing for literature what Freud was doing for psychoanalysis. Considering that both men seem to have seen sex as the basis for everything we think, feel and do, this was possibly quite near the mark. 'My subjects are love and death,' Schnitzler once said. 'What else is there to write about?' Schnitzler wrote many fine short stories. His best-known work is his play *Reigen* (known outside the German-speaking world as *La Ronde*), which provoked a week-long obscenity trial. When Hitler came to power, Schitzler's work was banned and burned. But he was in good company: books by Zweig, Freud and Einstein were consigned to the pyre as well.

Cécile Tormay (1875–1937): Born into a middle-class family in Budapest, the daughter of a vet, Tormay began writing at a young age. Her early influences were French and Italian writers. She shared the prejudices of many Hungarians of her class, as well as their terror of Bolshevism and their mistaken assumption that Mussolini and Fascism were the solution. She fiercely opposed the Communist government that took power in Hungary immediately after WWI and it was in the years immediately following the collapse of that government that she reached the height of her popularity. In 1922, at a time when Hungary was purging itself of political 'undesirables' in all branches of the arts, the Culture Minister offered her the editorship of *Napkelet* ('*Sunrise*'), a rival periodical to the famous *Nyugat* (meaning '*West*'—and by association, sunset and decadence). A controversial figure because of her Fascist-friendly politics and her anti-Semitism—as well as for her sexuality—the sun has now set on Cécile Tormay, a writer who was nominated more than once for the Nobel prize.

László Tóth (1889–1951): Tóth was born into the theatre, into a family of actors, the son of the director of the Hungarian National Theatre. He studied law in Hungary, Germany and France, and before WWI worked as a newspaper correspondent in Paris: many of his short stories draw on this experience. His Catholic faith was profound: he was involved in the organisation of the Vatican's World Exhibition of the Catholic Press in 1936 and led the Press office in 1937–8 for the Eucharistic conference held in Budapest. His world view inevitably led to him being expelled from the Hungarian Press Association when the Communists came to power. He was arrested, accused of treason and sentenced to ten years in prison with Cardinal Mindszenty, in the famous show trial. He died in captivity.

Stefan Zweig (1881–1942): Biographer, poet, essayist and short story writer, immersed in the literary life of Vienna, Zweig was a friend of Rilke and Roth, was greatly interested in Freud, and made use of the teachings of psychoanalysis in his historical biographies. Nazi persecution of Jews drove him to England, from where he later moved to Brazil. There, he became fatally depressed, being forced to confront the fact that the world he loved, a world where he had been successful and which had provided his entire cultural and intellectual hinterland, had ceased to exist. He eventually committed suicide, leaving behind a note, his *Declaração*, which concludes as follows: 'Greetings to all my friends! May they live to see the sunrise once again, after so long a night. I for my part, all too impatient, am going on ahead.' Zweig's posthumous novella *The Royal Game* uses chess as a symbol not only for Nazism but also as an extended metaphor for human existence, where men are mere pawns in the control of superior forces.

Notes

1. The Secession (p. 26) is a Vienna exhibition hall built in 1896–7 for the artistic movement of the same name, which broke away from Historicism and embraced a Jugendstil (Art Nouveau) aesthetic. It is home to Klimt's famous Beethoven frieze.
2. Auer lamps (p. 41) were a form of street lighting invented by the Austrian chemist Carl Auer, a pupil of Bunsen (of burner fame). The fragility of their filaments ultimately led to their being supplanted by electricity.
3. Währing (p. 68) was a suburb to the northwest of the city. It is now Vienna's District 18.
4. A straw boater (p. 68) was the trademark headgear of the comic actor and singer Alexander Girardi (1850–1918), a star of the Austrian stage.
5. The meal at Leidinger's (pp. 68–9) illustrates Silberer's economic superiority over Rudi. Leidinger's was a smart society restaurant on the Kärntnerstraße, right in the heart of Vienna. Here, Silberer feasts on beef and Bordeaux wine and smokes an expensive cigarette. Nestor Gianaclis was a Greek businessman who set up a tobacco factory in Cairo in 1871.
6. Anastasius Grün (p. 69) was the pen name of the politician and poet Count Anton Alexander von Auersperg (1806–76), an opponent of absolutist government. His bust does indeed stand in Vienna's Schillerplatz.
7. The Art Show (p. 70) was probably the huge exhibition organised as part of the 60th Jubilee celebrations for the emperor Franz Joseph in 1908. Alongside displays of art and crafts, there were gardens to stroll in and cafés offering food and drink.

8. Schrammel (p. 70) is a type of Austrian folk music, named after two 19th-century composers. It was (and still is) played in taverns and wine gardens. Schrammel bands feature a violin, a double-necked guitar, a clarinet and sometimes an accordion. Their catchy dance tunes, by turns merry and wistful, find echoes in the works of Classical composers such as Strauss.
9. The Stefanskeller (p. 70) was a popular cellar restaurant very close to the Stefansdom (St Stephen's Cathedral) in central Vienna.
10. The Sacher (p. 72), a famous luxury hotel and café Central Vienna famed for its *Sachertorte*, a cake made of chocolate and apricot jam.
11. The Melange (p. 72) is a popular Viennese way of making coffee, mixed with frothy milk. A *kipfel* is a crescent-shaped bread roll.
12. *Doboschtorte* (p. 73), a gateau invented by a late 19th-century Hungarian pastry chef, is composed of layers of sponge and chocolate and rum-flavoured cream with a hard caramel topping. Goldeck (p. 73) is an Austrian winery known for its sparkling wines, in production since 1859.
13. Wieden (p. 107) was a former suburb, south of the historic centre of Vienna. It is now the city's District 4.
14. Brünn (p. 121) is the Austrian name for Brno, formerly the capital of Moravia, now a city in the Czech Republic.
15. The Danube Kiosk (p. 127) was a coffee house with outdoor seating, near the Danube bank in Pest. It was in operation from the early 1880s until its demolition before the Second World War.
16. Kolozsvár (p. 127) is the Hungarian name for Cluj-Napoca, the unofficial capital of Transylvania, a region which was part of Hungary when this story was written. Known in German as Klausenburg, the city today belongs to Romania.
17. Vincze Skriván (p. 128) was a well-known hat maker who had his shop in central Pest, at the bottom of Váci utca, the main fashionable shopping street.

18. Ferenc Pórfi (p. 130) had a hat shop and gentlemen's outfitters at no. 8 Váci utca.
19. Váci Street (p. 133), in Hungarian 'Váci utca' (where both hat shops mentioned in this story were located), was the main shopping street for clothing, millinery, haberdashery etc. in late 19th-century Budapest. It retained its reputation until the end of the 20th century, when it became entirely known for its tourist outlets.
20. In the German wine world, Kabinett (p. 141) denotes a superior quality wine, the equivalent of a Reserve. All the wines on Lily's list are fine ones: Louis Roederer is a maker of notable champagne; Château Léoville is a well-known Bordeaux.
21. The type of head-dress referred to (p. 174) would have been similar to the lace-trimmed headband worn by a housemaid, tied around the crown of the head to keep the hair out of the eyes—and in this case with long tapes hanging down.
22. Badacsony (p. 183) is a volcanic wine region on the north shore of Lake Balaton. It is traditionally famed for a white wine made from the Kéknyelű grape.
23. The Nagykörút (p. 187) is a succession of wide boulevards running through central Pest: it is Budapest's equivalent of the Vienna Ringstrasse.
24. Géza Fejérváry (p. 217), an army officer and captain of the royal guard, was appointed Prime Minister by the emperor Franz Joseph in 1905, as an interim measure while Hungary's elected coalition found a way to tone down its virulently anti-Austrian, pro-independence ('1848-er') stance, which would have rendered the Dual Monarchy inoperable.